ANNAPURNA
A TREKKER'S GUIDE

Annapurna south from Machhapuchhare base camp.

ANNAPURNA
A TREKKER'S GUIDE

by

Kev Reynolds

CICERONE PRESS
MILNTHORPE, CUMBRIA, UK

A catalogue record for this book is available from the British Library.

This book is dedicated to the people of Nepal
who add a special dimension to every
visit made to their beautiful country.

PREFACE

I'd been involved in a love affair with mountains for thirty years and trekked in many different countries before I had an opportunity to visit Nepal. But that first visit sealed my fate; I would have to return - again and again and again. Those who are about to undertake their first visit must heed the warning: you may never settle, for the Himalaya can so easily become habit-forming.

Trekking in the Annapurna Himal will open your eyes not only to scenes of great beauty, but will enable you to build relationships with people of another race, another culture. How you interact, both with the country and the people, will depend upon the degree of sensitivity carried with you. The rewards you reap will derive directly from your willingness, or otherwise, to put Western values on hold and to give yourself to the multiplicity of experiences available and waiting there. Trekking in Nepal can be a feast. There's no need to go hungry.

Nepal holds so many opportunities for the trekker. This book is a guide to just one area - but what an area to concentrate on! Annapurna and its neighbouring peaks and valleys offer an arena for some of the most stimulating treks anywhere in the world. And it is my fervent hope that all who are drawn to this magnificent region, whether newcomers to trekking or old hands with years of experience behind them, will find as much magic there as I have whilst researching the trails for this book. But as you wander I urge you to treat the people and their landscapes with the respect and love they deserve. We have all heard of the Kleenex Trail; we all know a little about the environmental damage caused in the past, and the very real dangers that exist today with an ever-growing number of visitors. Those seemingly timeless mountains and valleys are delicate and vulnerable; so too are the cultures of those who live in their shadow. May each one of us add nothing to those problems, but instead help alleviate them.

In the words of the King Mahendra Trust for Nature Conservation: "While trekking, ponder your impact on the environment and culture. Teach people the importance of respecting nature and how to conserve it. By assisting in these small ways you will help Nepal enormously".

Trail information contained in this edition reflects as accurately as possible the routes as I found them. However, each monsoon adds its own signature to the landscape. Trails and bridges may be washed away and replaced elsewhere; villages grow, tea-houses and lodges multiply, and paths become re-routed. In order to improve and update future editions of this guide I would appreciate your help in providing a note of any changes found on trek, and also welcome comments or suggestions considered helpful to future trekkers. All notes and corrections sent to me via the publisher will be gratefully received.

It should be borne in mind that heights and distances quoted may not be entirely accurate. Different maps give varying figures and widely disparate spellings for some of the villages, mountains and passes. Until the perfect map is produced, accurately reflecting the contours of the land, we must be content with estimations. Times given for the various stages on trek are also estimates only, but are offered as a rough indication of the length of each day's walking. They do not allow for tea-house delays nor photographic interruptions, but are based on actual walking time.

This guidebook could not have been written without the help and encouragement of a number of people, especially those friends who generously supplied information before, during and after visits to Nepal. Others who shared the trails, tea-houses and lodges added much to the trekking experience and, often in unsuspecting ways, provided additional notes for inclusion. I gratefully acknowledge their contributions. Firstly, I am indebted as ever to my wife who kept the home together and paid the bills while I spent many weeks wandering in the Himalaya - no-one could ask for better support than she gives. In particular I wish to thank Roland Hiss, with whom the original outline of this book was conceived and who made many valuable suggestions in advance; my old trekking partner Alan Payne walked the Circuit with me and provided welcome route notes when our trails divided, as well as pointing out numerous incidental items for inclusion. He also read parts of the manuscript and made valuable suggestions for its improvement, which only adds to my sense of gratitude. Thanks also to Julian Bass for his advice and offers of further help; to Steve and Debbie Wilson, Ray and Lynda Knight, Bob and Bridget Vagedes and Steven van der Waals who shared some of the best days in the mountains; to Dendi Sherpa for his broad smiles and snippets of "inside" information, and to Sondru Gurung of Chhomrong who rescued an "Old Man - Very Tired" and challenged the sun with his laughter. I am grateful to them all.

Kev Reynolds

CONTENTS

Advice to Readers

Readers are advised that whilst every effort is taken by the author to ensure the accuracy of this guidebook, changes can occur which may affect the contents. It is advisable to check locally on transport, accommodation, shops etc but even rights-of-way can be altered and, more especially overseas, paths can be eradicated by landslip, forest fires or changes of ownership.

The publisher would welcome notes of any such changes

INTRODUCTION

Nepal is there to change you, not for you to change Nepal.

Approaching Kathmandu by air from India the plane swings eastward and suddenly, out of the left-hand window, a great bank of clouds hangs as a breaking wave of cumulus far above the brown wrinkled earth. At least, they look like clouds. Then you realise those clouds are rising out of clouds and they're not clouds at all. They're mountains - huge mountains plastered with ice and snow - savage fangs and gentle domes, lengthy crests and plunging faces, fins and spurs and buttresses drawing shadow. A long wall of mountains like a sawblade, pristine white and glistening in the sun; a serrated, castellated horizon, fortress-like and magnificent...

The Himalaya, kingdom of the snows: dream-world for many, reality for some. Once experienced they can never be forgotten, never dismissed from memory whether one's experience of them is in climbing to their summits or trekking through their valleys. Once seen they become a part of you, habit-forming and intrusive.

The Himalaya, of course, contain the youngest and highest mountains on earth - mountains that are still growing, that are spread in a monstrous chain reaching from Nanga Parbat in Pakistan to Namche Barwa in eastern Tibet - a fabulous wall of mountains with the peaks of fourteen of them rising above 8000 metres (26,000ft). Nepal boasts eight of these giants: Everest and Kanchenjunga, Lhotse, Makalu, Dhaulagiri, Manaslu, Cho Oyu and Annapurna.

Annapurna, first of the 8000-metre summits to be climbed and now the focus of some of the world's most exciting and visually spectacular treks.

Seen from the lakeside town of Pokhara in central Nepal the northern horizon, less than 40 kilometres (25 miles) away, is a swell of snow-capped peaks of the Annapurna Himal. Early morning they catch the first stain of sunrise and hover like a dream. Glorious mountains they are, full of promise and deep enchantment. Among them twelve summits rise in excess of 7000 metres (23,000ft) with a number of others more than 6000 metres (19,500ft) high. It's an island block moated on the east by the cleft of the Marsyangdi Khola and on the west by the deep Kali Gandaki valley. To the north, beyond the

Manang Himal and frontier ranges which form the northern wall of the curving Marsyangdi, lies Tibet. East of the Marsyangdi rises Manaslu (8163m: 26,781ft) and to the west of the Kali Gandaki the dramatic Dhaulagiri Himal crowned by the shapely ice peak of Dhaulagiri (8167m: 26,795ft) itself, while draining the heartland of this huge block of mountains is the deep shaft of the Modi Khola.

Apart from the mountains that dominate every scene, the Annapurna region represents one of the most geographically diverse areas imaginable. There are sub-tropical forests inhabited by monkeys, glorious hillsides ablaze with rhododendron or poinsettias, jungles of bamboo, upland pastures and pinewoods reminiscent of the Alps - and beyond the rain-shadow of the mountains, high, arid valleys and barren, windswept plateaux not unlike those found just to the north in Tibet.

This book is a guide to trekking in the Annapurna region. It describes the lengthy challenge of the Annapurna Circuit; the shorter, but visually rewarding, Annapurna Sanctuary trek; and thirdly, the Pilgrim's Trail to Muktinath which heads upvalley along the Kali Gandaki after first crossing the Poon Hill Danda with its justifiably famous sunrise views of Dhaulagiri and the Annapurnas. And it also makes suggestions for other treks and variations.

Each of these will reward the visitor with stunning panoramas, with an unbelievable variety of scenic wonders - from the lush vegetation of the lowlands where rice paddies terrace the foothills, to the arctic-like savagery of ice-falls and gleaming glaciers - and will surprise the newcomer to Nepal with the broad smiles and genuine open-hearted friendliness of the local people. *Namaste* is in their eyes and on their lips, and signs over lodge doorways that proclaim Wel-Come, mean just that.

If it is a dream of mountains that initially lures you to this Himalayan kingdom, it will be the valleys and hillsides populated by a wide range of ethnic groups, each united by a common bond of traditional Nepalese hospitality and cheerfulness, that ensures you do not forget it. Among the Annapurna massif the cultural diversity, the ethnic variety, is probably greater than anywhere else in all

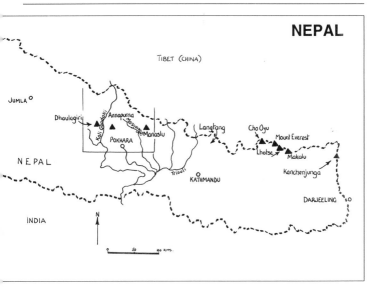

Nepal. A rich and memorable experience indeed awaits all prospective trekkers in the Annapurna Himal.

LANDSCAPE OF DREAMS

If there be a Paradise on earth, it is now, it is now, it is now!
(Wilfred Noyce)

Noyce had climbed to the South Col of Everest in 1953, and four years later was given the unique opportunity to attempt Machhapuchhare. He was a poet as well as a mountaineer, and his outpouring of emotion quoted above is echoed in the hearts of many who have the privilege of gazing at these glorious mountains. Every year tens of thousands of trekkers do just that.

Such a statistic may horrify you. You may imagine immense crowds of trekkers and their porters queueing to march through a village or to cross a narrow suspension bridge, of overloaded lodges and squalid, cramped campsites and broad eroded trails knee-deep

11

in litter. Happily the reality is not quite like that.

The Annapurna region covers an area of more than 2600 square kilometres (1000sq miles), and the main trekking seasons amount to about five months of the year. Although it would be wrong to suggest that there is no problem of numbers, there's time and space enough to swallow most of the crowds.

But clearly with so many visitors the potential for environmental damage is enormous, and over the years people-pressure has brought various problems, among them deforestation, pollution and cultural decay. However, with the efforts of the management and staff of the Annapurna Conservation Area Project (ACAP - established in 1986 under the auspices of the King Mahendra Trust for Nature Conservation) a programme of conservation linked with sustainable development has been set in motion with the aims of both repairing damage caused in the past, and preventing further environmental and cultural decline in the future.

It obviously behoves all who visit this magical region, whether on a brief once-only stroll through the foothills, or on a lengthy trek or climbing expedition, to treat both the landscape and those that live in it, with sensitivity and respect born of love.

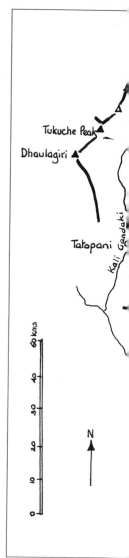

THE AREA OF THE ANNAPURNA TREKS

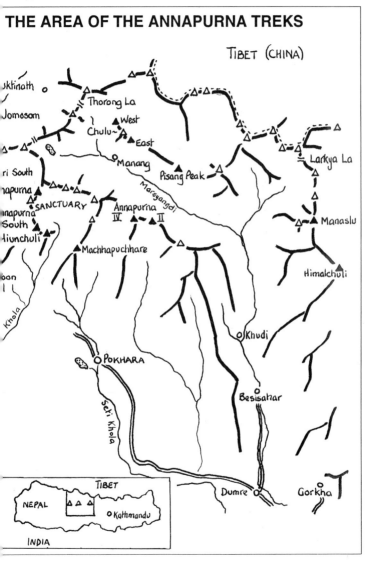

ANNAPURNA TREKS

This was the Himalaya, our promised land, and from now onwards
we would carry this vision with us wherever we went.
(Maurice Herzog)

The country north of Pokhara is, indeed, a promised land and the three main treks described in this guide provide ample opportunities to capture that vision in all its glory. Each has its own special appeal and its own rewards.

The Annapurna Circuit:

This is *the* classic trek, a three-week journey that makes a gigantic loop of the island block of the Annapurnas and follows about 200 kilometres (125 miles) of ancient trails. The ethnic and cultural diversity experienced throughout this journey is well-known, but it is matched by an astonishing array of vegetation and highlighted by an unfolding landscape of scenic riches.

Beginning to the east of Pokhara, either in Dumre or Gorkha, the trail heads north along the valley of the Marsyangdi, and reaches Manang in five to seven days. Manang sits in the rain-shadow of the Himalaya and gazes across the valley to a superb wall of mountains - the northern wall of the Annapurna Himal. Above the village begins the climb to the Thorong La, the crux of the trek at 5415 metres (17,766ft). Under snow-free, calm weather conditions the only difficulties lie in its height and the distance to cover between Phedi on the eastern side and Muktinath on the west. But in snow or extreme cold the Thorong La is a major obstacle; never should the seriousness of its crossing be under-estimated.

Once over the Thorong La the route descends to the upper valley of the Kali Gandaki, known here as the Thak Khola, by way of the pilgrim site of Muktinath, and begins the long southerly trek that leads between Dhaulagiri and the western slopes of the Annapurna massif - through the deepest valley on earth. This section of the walk gradually trades arid, Tibetan-like landscapes for dramatic scenes reminiscent of the Alps - but on a much larger scale. Then, below Tatopani, the Kali Gandaki is left behind in order to cross the terraced slopes of the Poon Hill Danda at the saddle of Ghorapani, before making the final descent of two or three days over a still-wrinkled land to Pokhara.

It is indeed a classic trek and a justifiably popular one, equally suited to tented, organised groups with their caravans of porters, as to independent trekkers relying on tea-houses and lodges for food and accommodation. There are plenty of lodges along the way, but above Manang bedspace is severely limited during the height of the season. On the Kali Gandaki side standards of accommodation are somewhat more advanced than those found along the Marsyangdi.

The Annapurna Sanctuary:

The Sanctuary is the name given by J.O.M. "Jimmy" Roberts to the central core of the almost complete circle of peaks he first explored in 1956. It is a fabulous amphitheatre whose sole access route is through the narrow, steep-walled and heavily-vegetated gorge of the Modi Khola. It was in the heartland of this Sanctuary that the only expedition ever sanctioned to attempt Machhapuchhare had its base in 1957, and from which Chris Bonington's expedition climbed the South Face of Annapurna in 1970. It makes a natural and rewarding objective for a trek setting out from Pokhara, and will require a minimum of ten days for the round-trip, depending on the actual route chosen.

Near the head of the Modi Khola's gorge the trail crosses an area threatened by avalanche, and bearing this danger in mind under certain conditions the route is impassable. It is particularly hazardous in winter and early spring, but heavy snowfall at any time of the year can close the Sanctuary for several days.

It is a spectacular walk, rather more demanding than some trekking companies like to suggest in their brochures, but somewhat less strenuous than the Annapurna Circuit outlined above.

From Pokhara the route heads roughly north-west to Dhampus on a foothill ridge among terraces of rice, millet or barley and with glorious views to the mountains. The way into the Modi Khola goes via Landrung and on to Chhomrong after a descent to, and steep climb from, the river. Two days of narrow helter-skelter trails lead through the gorge, finally emerging to the wonderland that is the Sanctuary, a spectacular cauldron of ice-coated mountains, namely: Hiunchuli, Annapurna South, Baraha Shikhar (Fang), Annapurna I, Gangapurna, Annapurna III, Gandharba Chuli and the graceful

15

fish-tail peak, Machhapuchhare - one of the most beautiful mountains in the world. In the Sanctuary itself there are two lodge areas offering seasonal accommodation: Machhapuchhare Base Camp (3703m: 12,149ft) and Annapurna Base Camp (4130m: 13,550ft), the latter a cold, often windy place, but providing an incredible 360 degree panorama of mountain majesty.

The Pilgrim's Trail to Muktinath:

The easiest and most popular of the three treks described, this is a linear route along the valley of the Kali Gandaki where the only possibility of varying the route back to Pokhara lies near its southern end. But it is a beautiful walk nonetheless, and with several interesting side trips possible. It is a trek that charts an ever-changing series of landscapes, a steadily-evolving range of vegetation, and experiences the riches of cultural diversity for which the region is noted.

Basically the trek reverses the second half of the Annapurna Circuit by crossing the Poon Hill Danda near Ghorapani and thereafter follows the course of the Kali Gandaki upvalley through Jomosom and on to Muktinath. This will make a round-trip of at least two weeks. Jomosom has a STOL (Short Take-Off and Landing) airstrip with flights to and from Pokhara - weather permitting.

As with both the Circuit and Sanctuary treks, the Pilgrim's Trail is well suited to those travelling without tents and porters and relying entirely on lodge accommodation. The Thakalis who live in the Kali Gandaki valley are among the most adept hoteliers in Nepal, and their lodges, guest-houses and hotels provided along this trail offer some of the best facilities for trekkers in all the Himalaya.

TREKKING AND TREKKING STYLES

Happiness is most often met by those who have learned to live in every moment of the present; none has such prodigal opportunities of attaining that art as the traveller. (T.G.Longstaff)

For Longstaff's "traveller" read "trekker" for trekking is more than travelling; trekking is taking part, being actively involved in a journey of discovery. Whereas the modern traveller is too often dependent on third-party schedules and mechanical aid, the trekker chooses to go where wheeled, mechanised transport is either rare, or completely unknown, and where walking is the only way to get from A to B. In such activity an almost constant sense of awareness becomes not only possible, but is highly desirable.

Where better to go trekking than in the Annapurna Himal?

But no-one should expect a wilderness experience for there are villages throughout - except for the stretch above Manang heading over the Thorong La to Muktinath, and beyond Chhomrong leading into the Sanctuary - and the well-walked trails have been in use for generations by local people carrying on trade with neighbouring villages on all sides of the Annapurna range. It may not be a wilderness experience, but trekking here gains by daily contact with the Nepalese and Tibetan mountain folk who populate the valleys.

Trekking comes in a variety of forms. There's the organised trek, when a group travels under the auspices of a commercial agency (adventure travel company). There's independent trekking, where two or three friends forego the company of porters or guides, travel light and use tea-houses and lodges throughout - sometimes referred to as "tea-house trekking". And there's a third course, a cross between independent and group travel, when a porter-guide is employed to carry one's gear and guide the trekker along the trail, using lodges for overnight accommodation. Few regions of the Himalaya offer better facilities to accommodate trekkers of all persuasions than does that of Annapurna.

Choice of trekking style for each individual will depend upon many considerations, such as cost, personal experience of mountain travel, availability of like-minded friends with whom to undertake a journey, amount of time required to organise and carry out the trek, choice of route etc. The following paragraphs therefore discuss options available, giving particular regard to the Annapurna region.

Trekking with an Adventure Travel Company:

This is the main choice for those with more money than time, for those who dislike the hassles of organisation, who get frustrated with bureaucracy, or who have limited mountain experience and want a degree of security. Trekking with a reputable adventure travel company does away with almost all pre-departure worries and trek concerns. Read the brochures and all dossiers carefully, sign the

17

form, make out your cheque and let someone else take care of the arrangements.

On a group trek porters carry all camping equipment, food, kitchen stores, personal baggage etc., leaving the trekker to shoulder just a light rucksack containing a few items likely to be required during the day. Nights are spent in tents; all meals are prepared and served by a staff of trained Nepalese cooks and kitchen boys, latrines are dug by paid staff, tents erected and dismantled for you, and "Sherpa" guides ensure that you do not get lost along the trail. A sirdar takes overall responsibility for the smooth running of the trek, but usually a Western leader also accompanies the group to act as liaison officer between trekkers and the local staff. This leader often has an understanding of any medical problems likely to be encountered, and has charge of a comprehensive medical kit. Some companies also offer financial incentives to encourage qualified medical personnel to accompany a trek on a particular route.

A skilled trek cook can provide a surprising variety of meals using just basic portable equipment. And, of considerable importance, the standard of hygiene can be controlled; therefore the health of members of an organised party is likely to be better than that of trekkers relying solely on tea-houses and lodges along the way.

It's a very sociable way to travel, particularly for those who have no like-minded friends with whom to share an active holiday. Daily you will be walking with people you may never have met before, and many lasting relationships develop from on-trek introductions. On the other hand you may well find that there are some in the party you'd rather not have met, although groups are usually of sufficient size (10-14 is normal) to enable you to avoid too close contact with anyone whose personality rubs against your own. Each year hundreds of trekkers resolve to undertake new journeys with a travel company they've learned to trust. Adventure travel companies regularly advertise in the outdoor press, and a number organise promotional evenings in the winter when slides of a variety of treks are shown and prospective customers have an opportunity to meet and question trek leaders - a good way to assess what is on offer.

Organised parties, of course, generally need to keep to a pre-determined route and maintain a fairly strict schedule, which can be a little annoying if you see an enticing side valley you'd like to visit.

On the other hand, since each day's stage is limited by the distance a heavily-laden porter can cover, the journey is made at a fairly leisurely pace, thus allowing plenty of time to enjoy the scenery and indulge in photography along the way.

Whilst group travel tends to insulate its members from interaction with local people, trekking for two weeks or more in the company of Nepalese guides, cooks and porters gives a marvellous opportunity, for those so inclined, to build a relationship that can be immensely rewarding for all concerned.

On an organised trek the day begins with a mug of tea brought to your tent at around 6 o'clock, closely followed by a bowl of hot water for washing. Breakfast is eaten soon after; in low country this will be outside around a table with views of the distant mountains and hills warming to the new day. In higher, colder country, a mess tent will be used.

The day's trek starts early, around 7.30am when the light is pure, the air cool and birds active. The trek crew will break camp and the army of porters pack their *dokos* (large baskets in which equipment or goods are carried) and set off along the trail. Sometime during the morning's walk the kitchen crew will rattle past and set up their cooker in a selected spot for lunch. This may be eaten any time between 11.00am and 1.00pm, usually a hot meal with plenty of liquids.

The afternoon's walk will finish at around 4 o'clock, giving the chance to write journal notes, read a book or chat with other members of the group while camp is being set up and the evening meal prepared. This meal is usually finished by 6.30 or 7 o'clock allowing plenty of time to rest, read, talk or listen to the songs of the Sherpas under a starlit sky.

Independent Trekking:

For those who enjoy, or are not averse to making all arrangements, such as organising visas, booking flights and hotels in Kathmandu, queuing for permits, buying bus tickets to Pokhara, route-finding on trek, choosing meals and lodges - independent tea-house trekking is the answer. It can be a very rewarding way to travel, but it is essential to adopt a flexible attitude of mind and be ready to adapt to a wide variety of circumstances. There'll be no-one to blame when things go wrong, for every decision made is your own. But it is also the cheapest way to trek in Nepal.

Tea-house trekking is very popular in the Annapurna region, for there are lodges and/or tea-houses offering food or shelter practically every hour along the way on each of the treks described in this book, thus enabling you to travel with a minimum amount of equipment.

So far as this guidebook is concerned, a tea-house is a trailside building that offers basic refreshment to travellers; a lodge is a simple hotel (*bhatti*) where both food and shelter are provided. These *bhatti* are variously advertised as guest-houses, inns, hotels or lodges, but whatever the sign says outside, standards of accommodation are fairly basic - although there will inevitably be some places offering a higher degree of comfort than others. It should also be explained that provision for trekkers is undergoing constant change and steady improvement with the encouragement of ACAP.

At the time of writing most lodges consist of a simple building comprising kitchen, dining area and an assortment of twin-bedded rooms. Some have dormitory accommodation too. Washing facilities may be no more than a stand-pipe out in the yard, cold water being the norm. A few offer hot showers, but these "showers" are rarely anything more than a hosepipe in an outhouse with luke-warm water provided. Toilets are usually a simple outbuilding with a hole in the floor above a pit. Although standards are improving, some of these toilets are primitive enough to make you yearn for constipation. Sleeping quarters consist of a small bare room, which is little more than a cell, furnished with two firm, but small beds. There is no floor covering and, at best, there will only be a nail or two in the walls from which to hang clothing or towels. Beds are provided with a thin foam-rubber mattress and usually a pillow. Trekkers are advised to carry and use an insulation mat (Karrimat or similar) for additional comfort and as a prevention against possible infestation from some of the mattresses provided. Walls are very thin and are not soundproof.

On environmental grounds lodge-keepers in the ACAP region are encouraged to change from wood fires to kerosene burners for cooking. Trekkers should applaud this, for apart from the obvious impact on the environment, in those lodges where cooking is still by open fire woodsmoke often finds its way through the floor boards of bedrooms located directly above the kitchen area. Dining rooms are usually poorly lit, but in the best of them a convivial atmosphere is easily created - especially in the higher regions where a brazier of hot coals is placed beneath the table as a form of central heating and trekkers huddle together for warmth of an evening.

Bhattis offer a surprising choice of meals. Trekkers who arrive expecting to exist on a diet of *daal bhaat* three times a day will be pleasantly surprised by the size and variety of lodge menus - although it should be stressed that not all items listed will always be available. Pizzas and apple pies are not at all uncommon in the Annapurna region, so you can vary your diet between Western and traditional Nepali food if desired. One thing should be made clear; many *bhattis* have an over-ambitious choice of meals available, but only one fire on which to cook. It follows then, that if the lodge or tea-house is busy and trekkers order a wide variety of meals, you can find yourself waiting literally hours to be served. Not only can this be frustrating (particularly if you're hungry after a long day's walk), it also means that more firewood than necessary is being used. Try to assess what your fellow trekkers are ordering and follow their lead.

The standard procedure on arrival at a lodge is to enquire of the owner if there are vacancies, and if so request a padlock to secure your room. Find out what and where washing and toilet facilities there are, and if there is a set time by which meals need to be ordered. After ordering, you are normally expected to enter details of room number and meals taken in a book provided especially for this purpose. All food and drinks served during the stay are similarly entered in this book and payment made on departure. Trekkers are often trusted to add up the cost of each item ordered (listed on the house menu) themselves, and pay the correct total; please do not betray the trust placed upon you. Prices are exceedingly modest by Western standards, and the cost of a room so low that the lodge keeper relies on selling meals and drinks to make a reasonable living. Do not book a bed at one lodge and eat in another. Bear in mind that all goods must be carried on the backs of porters, often for many days at a time, so it follows that prices increase in proportion to distance from a road.

Independent trekkers staying in lodges along the way are able to enjoy a much more flexible routine than those on an organised trek, and can vary their route according to taste. Even more so than on an organised trek, it is an extremely sociable way of journeying among the mountains, although there is a danger of mixing only with fellow Western trekkers and so missing out on the chance to enrich your travels by a closer contact with Nepalese villagers. But for those who wish to learn more about local people, customs and the life of villages along the route, opportunities abound. However, the best way to enjoy cultural interaction is with the third method of trekking, that is, with a porter-guide.

Trekking with a Porter-Guide:

This can prove to be extremely rewarding and enlightening, for the best Nepalese porter-guides can quickly become your trusty friends and companions who provide a daily insight into the ways of the people whose country you are travelling through. A porter-guide will carry some of your gear, make sure you keep on the correct trail and act as a link between yourself and locals met on the path. Those who are really familiar with the region you're journeying through may suggest interesting diversions to side valleys or to villages off the route of most Western trekkers. They can teach you so much of value and, if you are sensitive, keen to learn and prepared to treat your companion as a friend rather than a servant, your experience will be the more profound as a result. There is the additional assurance that you are providing welcome employment too, and it is worth remembering that the role of porter is by no means a demeaning one, for it has long formed a major source of employment throughout the hill regions of Nepal.

The hiring of porter-guides may be arranged in Kathmandu, either privately or through one of the many trekking agencies based in the city. (Beware of picking a "guide" off the streets.) For greater flexibility it is sometimes possible to hire one along the route, either for a day or two, or for the duration of the trek. If you choose the latter course, enquire of your lodge keeper for a reputable local man - preferably one who speaks a modicum of English. Porter-guides hired in Kathmandu will invariably speak some English; many are Khumbu region Sherpas. Payment is usually based on a set fee per day, inclusive of food and lodging, or a higher wage with the requirement that the porter provides his own food.

Once you hire a man, of course, you assume employer's responsibility for his well-being. This includes making sure he is adequately clothed and equipped to cope with below-freezing temperatures if your proposed route reaches high altitudes (as on the Annapurna Circuit or into the Sanctuary). A porter-guide hired through a reputable Kathmandu agency may be expected to be well-equipped, but if you take on an inexperienced man from the sub-tropical lowlands he could be ignorant of the degree of cold likely to be encountered on the Thorong La, for example, so you must satisfy yourself that he has adequate footwear and warm clothing. If he does not have certain items, it is up to you to supply them.

The easiest and most lightweight form of trekking with a porter-guide relies on the use of lodges for accommodation. Once you decide to camp, of course, you enter a more complicated style, with a leaning towards the organised trek. The more equipment you need the more porters you will require to carry it. In Kathmandu there are plenty of agencies that can supply the manpower and equipment needed.

One final point: trekking alone is not recommended. Although Nepal is one of the friendliest countries you could ever wish to visit, it has not escaped some aspects of Western civilisation and crime is no longer entirely unknown. Regrettably some solitary trekkers have been mugged and a few have even disappeared on lonely sections of some of the busiest trails. If you prefer not to travel in an organised group and have no friend to trek with, do consider hiring a porter-guide.

ON TREK

Take nothing but photos, leave nothing but footprints,
kill nothing but time.
(Much-quoted slogan that has become the wilderness mantra.)

One of the saddest sights I remember from days around Annapurna was the bewildered face of a Nepali being berated by a Western trekker for failing to understand a demand for food at a tea-house that had no food for sale. The tea-house owner had every reason to feel confused and hurt; the trekker had no cause either to demand anything of the Nepali, nor especially to curse him for his failure to understand. Ignorance was the trekker's lesser crime; his bad manners were unforgiveable.

We are all innocents abroad. Our culture in the West is no preparation for the kaleidoscopic cultures of the East, but it is an arrogance to imagine that ours is superior to theirs. We can probably learn more from our Nepalese hosts with regard to living in contentment than they can from us. Their culture has developed separately from ours, and observation of its intricacies is an important ingredient in successful trekking. As uninvited guests in Nepal it is up to each one of us to do our best to understand and respect the ways of our hosts. So there are certain rules of behaviour that every trekker should learn before setting out on a journey to this magical Himalayan kingdom in order to avoid acts of inadvertent disrespect.

Affection: Avoid public displays of affection.

Begging: In general don't encourage it. Discourage children who beg for school pens, balloons, money or candy. However, it is acceptable to give a few rupees to a *sadhu* on pilgrimage.

Campfires: Conserve wood. Resist the temptation to have a campfire, and only cook on kerosene stoves. When using lodges, reduce the demand for hot showers except where water is solar heated.

Dress: A state of undress is unacceptable. Don't be seen without a shirt; neither should women wear shorts. Women should wear a long skirt or slacks, and should never be seen in revealing blouses.

Food: You should not touch food or utensils that Nepalis will use. Never give or take food with the left hand.

Haggling: Whilst haggling is part of the trade culture of Kathmandu and Pokhara, never haggle over prices in tea-houses or lodges on trek. Prices are listed on menus and are set by the local community.

The hearth: Do not discard rubbish into your host's fire, nor sit next to it in a Nepali home unless invited to do so.

Legs & feet: The soles of your feet should never be pointed at a Nepali, nor should legs be so outstretched that they need to be stepped over to pass. Nepalis will not step over legs or feet.

Litter: Do not leave litter - anywhere.

Monasteries: When visiting monasteries remove your shoes before entering, and leave a donation before leaving.

Photography: Be discreet when taking photographs of buildings and local people. Remember, you are not in a zoo, nor in a museum. Ask permission before taking photographs of people, and respect their right to say no.

Prayer walls: Always pass to the left of prayer walls and chortens.

Smile: Act with patience and friendliness towards Nepalese people - and smile. The Nepalese smile a lot. That warmth should be reflected back.

Toilets: No matter how unhealthy some may seem, do make use of the toilet facilities provided. If it is completely unavoidable and you must defecate where no toilet is available, always bury your faeces well away from water courses and burn used toilet paper.

Touching: Never touch a Nepali on the head; and do not touch anyone with your shoes.

Wealth: Be discreet when handling money; do not tempt locals into envy by making an obvious display of the contents of your wallet. Keep a few small rupee notes handy for paying bills along the way. Don't leave valuable items unattended.

Finally, the word *Namaste*, given with hands pressed together, is the universal greeting of Nepal; it means "I salute the God within you" and will be well-received when offered to a Nepali on trail, in villages or in lodges and tea-houses. Use it with a smile - and mean it. From such simple beginnings may grow a flower of understanding.

TREKKING SEASONS

The greatest drawback to climbing in monsoon conditions,
greater even than the bad visibility, is the high temperature.
(H.W.Tilman)

Two major seasons are suitable for trekking in the Annapurna region: spring (pre-monsoon) and autumn (post-monsoon). The most popular is the autumn period of late September to early December when skies are mostly clear and weather patterns generally settled with little rainfall. However, at high altitudes snow can fall at any time, and those who set out on the Annapurna Circuit, or intend visiting the Sanctuary during this time should be adequately equipped with warm clothing and good-quality sleeping bags. It may be an obvious point to make, but there is a marked difference between one's acceptance of cold when moving, and when resting.

From December to February both days and nights turn very cold in the mountains, snowfall can be expected above 2000 metres (6500ft) and an attempt to cross the Thorong La can be fraught with danger (mainly from cold and a build-up of snow), while the route through the valley of the Modi Khola should be avoided because of avalanche threat - this danger is especially serious in late winter and early spring. Many lodges are also closed in winter.

The spring trekking season runs from March to May. Temperatures can be very warm in the lower valleys, rain showers and storms are not uncommon and there is an accumulation of haze that often obscures afternoon views; but the wild flowers - notably forests of rhododendron - create marvellous banks of colour on the approach to the big mountains. It is also a prime time for bird watchers.

June to mid-September marks the period of monsoon rains. In the northern half of the range, including Manang and Jomosom, valleys nestle in the rain-shadow of the Himalaya, but the southern slopes are daily awash with rainstorms that can cause flooding, landslides and on occasion even broken bridges. It is hot and humid at low altitudes and the lowlands are plagued with mosquitoes too. Trails are muddy and infested with leeches, and views severely limited. However, those who have braved the monsoon months speak of the drama of swirling clouds that suddenly part to reveal snow-dashed mountains, and of the pleasure of virtually tourist-free villages on normally busy trails. They tell of lush greenery and a bountiful vegetation as well as the horror of heat and mud, of wading swollen rivers, of treacherous paths and of burning leeches from legs and arms.

PERMITS AND VISAS

*Never expect any encouragement from the government
of your country.* (Lord Curzon)

Citizens of all countries, except India and Bhutan, will require a valid passport and tourist visa to enter the country. Visa applications should be made direct to the Nepalese Embassy or Consulate in your home country (addresses are listed in the Appendix). This is a straight-forward process that involves minimal form filling, the provision of two passport photographs and the payment of a fee (check current prices with the Embassy). Postal applications should be made at least a month before departure. The visa is valid for a period of three months after the date of issue and has a duration of 30 days.

A 30-day visa is also now available on entry at Kathmandu airport. Two further extensions of a month each may be obtained for most visas, but after three months in Nepal you will be expected to leave the country for at least one month before being allowed to return. Extensions may be purchased at the Central Immigation Office on Tridevi Marg (between Kantipath and Thamel) and in Pokhara at the Central Immigration Office near Damside. Applications must be accompanied by passport, passport photographs and photocopies of bank exchange receipts. Instant photo facilities and photocopying machines are found near the Immigration Offices in both Kathmandu and Pokhara.

A trekking permit is also required for all treks in the Annapurna region, as is payment of 200 rupees for entry to the Annapurna Conservation Area (necessary for all routes described in this guidebook). A trekking fee, based on the number of days for which you require a permit, is levied on application. Permits are issued by the Central Immigration Office in Kathmandu and also in Pokhara. Offices are open Sunday to Thursday 10.00am to 2.00pm, and Friday morning from 10.00 to noon. But beware of the many official holidays and festivals that occur with some frequency and can leave you kicking your heels for days whilst waiting for the office to re-open. In the main trekking season queues are exceedingly long and progress seems dreadfully slow. However, the clerks dealing with an avalanche of applications work under considerable pressure and need your understanding, not expressions of frustration. (When tempted to curse the bureaucratic form filling and long hours spent standing in queues, consider the treatment handed out to certain foreign nationals by some immigration officials at major airports in the U.K. and other Western capitals.)

Application forms for trekking permits are available at the entrance to the Immigration Office where a list of current rules and regulations is posted. In addition to your passport with valid visa, you will currently require two passport photographs and photocopies of bank receipts showing that you have changed at least 20 U.S. dollars for each day you will be on trek. Be warned that regulations change from time to time. On trek you will regularly need to have your permit checked at the police posts situated at intervals along the trail, so do not think you can short-cut the system and trek without.

Permit applications can usually be dealt with the same day (check what time you must return to collect it), but in the busiest times, apparently, it may be necessary to wait up to three days before permits are ready.

If you are trekking with an adventure travel company, your agent will no doubt arrange permits and visa extensions on your behalf. In both Kathmandu and Pokhara it is possible that you will be offered permits and visas on the black market, but you are strongly urged to resist the temptation. Westerners have languished in Nepalese jails with plenty of time to regret having done so. The official fees you pay for the privilege of trekking in Nepal are, after all, an important source of income for one of the poorest countries in the world.

PRE-DEPARTURE PREPARATIONS

The traveller's ambition often exceeds his powers of endurance.
(Karl Baedeker)

It is an interesting observation that the highest mountains in the world attract to their valleys numerous trekkers who may never have undertaken a multi-day walk before. That so many survive the experience to return for more says as much for the spell cast by the Himalaya as for the care and attention devoted to them by their trek organisers and crew.

Trekking demands mental preparation as much as physical fitness. Embarking upon a journey that will take two or three weeks to complete, is a very different proposition to that of a fortnight's holiday based in one village from which to set off on day walks whenever the mood arises. As a member of an organised group trek you will be expected to walk day after day, rain or shine, whether you feel up to it or not. Obviously real infirmity is excluded from this statement, but trail weariness is not. Get yourself both mentally and physically fit before boarding the plane to Kathmandu.

Consider the following scenario: of waking one morning weary from past excesses and feeling queasy from a stomach upset. Consider a cold wind and falling rain and a trek leader cajoling you to start walking. You have about eight hours of uphill trail ahead of you before the next camp is set up - and there's no alternative but to pull on boots and waterproofs and start walking.

High on the Annapurna Circuit there may well be extended periods of intense cold to put up with, of days without being able to have a decent wash, or several nights in a row when you've not been able to enjoy restful sleep. Maybe the diet is not to your liking or, if you're new to camping, you've discovered you don't like sleeping in a tent. On a tea-house trek you could be dismayed by the standard of accommodation provided. There will be times of confusion: times when your Western sensibilities are appalled by the different values accepted by those whose country you are wandering through. Successful trekking demands an ability to adapt to a whole range of ever-changing circumstances, to put Western values on hold and be prepared to accept that there could be much to learn from Nepali hill culture. Learning to respect an unfamiliar culture is in itself sometimes a shock to the system.

But if you're convinced that wandering through the most dramatic scenery on earth, of mingling daily with people of an entirely foreign culture, and that a sense of achievement at the end of the trek offer sufficient rewards for the odd day of misery - then trekking is for you. If you have any doubts, forget it. Five or six days into a long walk is not the time to decide that trekking is not your cup of tea. The financial outlay required to undertake a trek in Nepal should be sufficient spur to ensure that you enjoy every moment of your time there; don't waste it on doubts or inadequate preparation.

There's only one real way to get physically fit for trekking in the Himalaya, and that is by walking up and down hills. Jogging will help to build stamina and endurance, swimming and cycling are also of great benefit but uphill walking with a rucksack is the best possible preparation. If hills are in short supply near your home, just walk as often as you can wherever convenient. Once you arrive in the Annapurna foothills and the trail winds away before you, you'll be glad you put in some effort at home.

Having decided to go trekking in the Annapurna Himal, put most of your well-developed Western values behind you, open your eyes and your mind to all that Nepal has to offer, and set forth with a determination to see and to understand. As has been pointed out by a number of experienced trekkers in the past, few will be content with just one Himalayan journey. The "trek of a lifetime" is likely to be the first of many.

HEALTH MATTERS

Expect not to find things as at home, for you have left home to find things different. (The trekker's commandment.)

First-time visitors to the Himalaya often become obsessed with concerns about their health. In fact there are times when the trails of Nepal become hypochondriacs' highways. Conversations in tents and lodges alike zone in on topics related to bowel and bladder movement, on worries related to the digestive tract, about headaches, chest infections and fears of altitude sickness.

Clearly, the farther you wander from 'civilisation' the more important it is to look after your health, but don't let these concerns become obsessive. Prior to leaving home have those preventative innoculations deemed necessary by the health authorities, take a first aid kit with you, adopt a sensible attitude towards food and hygiene on trek - then chance to luck. Trekking overall is a healthy activity. Things will not be as they are at home, but if you expect there to be no risk at all in a Third World country, save your money or book a holiday elsewhere.

Nepal makes no requirement for visitors to show proof of vaccination or immunization, unless travelling by way of an infected area, but you are recommended to be vaccinated against the following: cholera, tuberculosis (BCG), typhoid, tetanus, meningitis and hepatitis. This last-named is given in the form of an injection of gamma-globulin as near to the date of departure as possible. Should your journey to Nepal pass through a region where yellow fever is prevalent, it will be necessary to be vaccinated against this also. If coming from a cholera or yellow fever infected area, you may need to show a valid certificate of innoculation on entry.

Rabies exists in Nepal and there is a slight chance that you might be bitten whilst on trek. You may wish to consider vaccination against this.

If you plan to visit the Terai, or travel by way of Bangladesh or India, you will be advised to embark on a course of anti-malaria tablets. Advice differs, depending on areas to be visited, but one may expect to take two Paludrin tablets daily, as well as two others (as advised) at weekly intervals. The course begins 24 hours before departure and continues for 28 days after your return home.

In addition to advice provided by your medical practitioner, up-to-date specialist health advice can be obtained in Britain from MASTA (Medical Advisory Services for Travellers Abroad) who will send printed information in response to a telephone request. There is a charge for this service. The number to call is: 071 631 4408 (between 09.30 and 17.00 Monday to Friday inclusive). Their address is: MASTA, Keppel Street, London WC1E 7HT.

Anyone suffering from lung or heart diseases should avoid treks that go to high altitudes, and should consult their doctor before commiting themselves to a trip to Nepal. It is in any case sensible to have a medical check before setting off on a lengthy Himalayan trek.

Coughs, colds and chest infections are prevalent and are exacerbated by smokey lodges and the dry cold air of high altitude. The sound of coughing and spitting is the hill music of Nepal. Soluble lozenges will soothe inflamed throats, catarrh pastilles are worth taking, as are antibiotics in the event of chest infections.

The main danger to health in Nepal though is through contracting disease from contaminated water. A variety of organisms live happily in the streams and rivers, including *giardia* cysts. All water in the country (including Kathmandu and Pokhara) should be considered suspect unless it has been vigorously boiled for ten minutes, treated with iodine or comes in a bottle with an unbroken seal. Other water purifying systems do not kill *giardia*. Iodine (Lugol's solution - available in Kathmandu pharmacies) should be carried in a small plastic dropper bottle; eight drops per litre is the recommended dose rate. Leave for 30 minutes before drinking. Many iodine bottles sold in Kathmandu have suspect screw tops, and you are advised to transfer the contents to a more leak-proof container.

If you are trekking with a group in the care of a reputable adventure travel company, the cook and kitchen crew will make every effort to ensure that all water is properly treated and you should have no concerns on this score. However, if you are relying on food and drink from tea-houses and lodges, you should be a little more circumspect. Drink only those liquids you can be sure have been adequately boiled - such as tea. Beware milk drinks. Coca Cola, Fanta and Nepalese bottled beers are available almost everywhere in the Annapurna region and should give no cause for health concern.

You should also remember that it is not only by drinking contaminated water that you can contract something nasty, but also by using it to clean your teeth. If you cannot be certain about the quality of the water available, do not rinse your teeth with it.

Safe bottled water is available almost everywhere in the Annapurna region (do not accept it if the seal has been broken); but since the bottles are made of plastic and have no further use after being emptied, there are certain environmental problems concerned with their disposal.

Food is another problem area for independent trekkers, but with a little forethought you should remain trouble-free. Try to avoid uncooked fruit (unless you can peel it yourself), salad vegetables that may have been rinsed in untreated water, and certain foods (such as lasagne) that have been cooked and later reheated. Lodge menus provide sufficient variety that most problems can be avoided. But even so, many trekkers suffer a dose of diarrhoea *(Kathmandu Quickstep)* at some time or other during their stay in Nepal, although often this is simply reaction to a change of diet. Sufferers should not become alarmed unless blood is passed in the stools (a sign of possible dysentery), for this usually remedies itself in a few days. Simply take plenty of liquids to prevent dehydration, reduce solid food intake and avoid dairy products and alcohol. A rehydration solution, such as Jeevan Jal (the Nepalese brand obtainable in Kathmandu and Pokhara) is quickly absorbed into the system and will help speed recovery.

Giardia lamblia is a protozoan parasite whose cyst is prevalent in the streams and even the dust of upland Nepal, and in the Annapurna

Above Bhulbhule the valley walls are streaked with cascades. (Circuit Stage 2)

The bridge at Syange (Circuit. Stage 3)
The gorge-cut trail above Bhratang (Circuit. Stage 5)

region trekkers seem to have a particular dread of contracting disease from it. It may take up to three weeks for symptoms to make themselves known after cysts have been unconsciously swallowed. One sure way of identifying a sufferer from *giardia* is by the foul-smelling, bad-egg gases emitted. Although not life-threatening, *giardia* is still a major health risk (and it strains friendships). Symptoms include nausea, stomach cramps, weight loss and dehydration. Irregular bouts of diarrhoea accompanied by mucus is also part of the symptom, but treatment is fairly rapid with the use of tinidazole - Tiniba is the brand name available in Kathmandu pharmacies. (It might be worth noting that *giardia* is now present also in parts of the United States, in New Zealand and South Africa; it is not limited to Third World countries.)

All food and drinks consumed in Kathmandu and Pokhara should be treated with the same circumspection as on trek. The time to relax completely with regard to meals and liquids is when you arrive home. That being said, do keep your concerns in perspective and don't allow them to dominate your time in Nepal. With a little forethought and detail to personal hygiene, you should remain perfectly fit and healthy.

Mountain Sickness:

The other major concern of trekkers is that of altitude, or mountain, sickness. Acute Mountain Sickness (AMS) can affect anyone above an altitude of about 2000 metres (6500ft), but it is not possible to predict in advance who will suffer from it. Physical fitness is of no apparent benefit, neither is youthfulness. In fact it would appear that young people may be more susceptible to AMS than are older trekkers.

AMS occurs as a result of the body failing to acclimatise adequately to reduced oxygen levels experienced at altitude. Nowhere in the Annapurna region is too high for a normal healthy body to acclimatise, given time, but some take much longer than others to adapt. By failing to allow sufficient time for acclimatisation, AMS is almost guaranteed to develop. The best way to avoid it is to ascend slowly once you reach 2000 metres (6500ft), and above 3000 metres (10,000ft) ascend no more than about 400 metres (1300ft) per day. On the Annapurna Circuit it is not easy to follow the golden rule of "climb high, sleep low" so it is important to make a gradual ascent, with rest days, in order to allow the body to acclimatise properly. Another important consideration is liquid intake. At altitude it is necessary to drink at least four litres (7 pints) a day in order to avoid dehydration, and to urinate a minimum of half a litre per day - a great deal of fluid is lost at altitude through breathing. Yellow-coloured urine is a sign that liquid intake needs to be increased.

With the onset of AMS fluid accumulates in the lungs or the brain or, in severe cases, in both. Recognition of the symptoms, and attention to reducing them, are both vital if serious illness or, at the worst, death is to be avoided. Early symptoms of mild AMS to watch for are extreme fatigue, headache and loss of appetite. Some trekkers also find themselves breathless with only minimal exercise, and suffer disturbed sleep. When these symptoms develop do not go any higher until they have gone away. If they show no sign of leaving after a day or two, but instead become worse, it is important to descend to lower levels. Do not take sleeping tablets nor strong pain killers at altitude, since these can mask some of the symptoms.

A worsening condition is indicated by vomiting, severe headache, lack of co-ordination, wet, bubbly breathing, increased tiredness and breathlessness even at rest. Such symptoms warn of the onset of a very serious condition which, if ignored, can lead to lack of consciousness and death within 12 hours. The only cure is to descend at once until symptoms decrease and finally disappear completely. An improvement will normally be felt after 300 metres (1000ft) or so of descent.

High Altitude Cerebral Edema (HACE) and High Altitude Pulmonary Edema (HAPE) occur as advanced stages of AMS and are both potential killers. Every year a number of trekkers die in Nepal through failure to recognise and respond to the symptoms. The only known cure is immediate descent to lower altitudes. In the case of HACE and HAPE no sufferer should be left to descend alone, neither should there be any delay. If symptoms occur at night do not even wait until morning to descend.

As with all health concerns, it is important to be aware of potential dangers, but keep them in perspective and do not allow your concerns to devalue the pleasures of the trek. Be aware of symptoms, act upon them if they occur and, time and energy willing, continue with your trek when signs of improvement indicate.

A medical aid post run by volunteers from the Himalayan Rescue Association is situated in Manang. Two doctors are in attendance during the main trekking seasons, and each afternoon they give a lecture, *Mountain Sickness and How to Avoid Dying From It*. This is well worth attending. They are also available for medical consultations. A fee is charged for consultations, but not for attendance at the lectures, although a donation will be most welcome.

There are hospitals at Besisahar, Jomosom and Pokhara, and medical posts at Ghandrung and Tatopani in addition to the one mentioned above in Manang. For emergency evacuation there are STOL airstrips at Hongde below Manang, and at Jomosom, but flights are dependent upon good weather conditions and should not be relied upon. Evacuation from more remote areas of the Annapurna region is difficult to organise and extremely expensive to carry through. Rescue takes time, there is a scarcity of radio communication and a shortage of helicopters available. Rescues will only be attempted when a guarantee of sufficient payment has been made. Independent trekkers stand little or no chance of having a positive response to a call for airlift evacuation from any remote region.

First Aid Kit:

All trekkers, whether travelling independently or with an organised group, should carry a personal first aid kit, the very minimum contents of which should be:

Elastoplast dressing strips	Moleskin (to prevent blisters)
Bandages (cotton gauze & elastic)	Aspirin (or Paracetamol)
Throat lozenges (& cough pastilles)	Thermometer
Iodine (in dropper bottle)	Sun cream
Immodium (or similar for diarrhoea relief)	Lip salve
Dioralyte (or Jeevan Jal for rehydration)	Antiseptic cream
Antibiotic (Ciproxin or as prescribed)	Tiniba (to combat *giardia*)
Scissors	Safety pins

Also recommended is a pack of sterile needles for use in emergencies where injections are necessary, in order to reduce the risk of accidental transmission of HIV (AIDS) and Hepatitis B viruses through contaminated equipment. MASTA (see above) produces a sterile medical equipment pack that contains syringes, sutures and dressings as well as needles.

Most medicines are readily available without prescription in Kathmandu. But you should not rely on the diagnostic advice of pharmacists; where doubts occur, seek medical assistance. Make sure you have all you might be expected to require in the way of medical aid before setting out on trek.

EQUIPMENT CHECK-LIST

A superabundance of luggage infallibly increases the delays, annoyances, and expenses of travel. To be provided with enough and no more, may be considered the second golden rule of the traveller. (Karl Baedeker)

It is perhaps as well that most airlines have a free baggage allowance of only 20kgs (44lbs), since there is a tendency by some group trekkers to take far too much clothing and equipment with them - knowing that with porters they will not have to carry it all themselves whilst on trek. Independent trekkers, on the other hand, will recognise the necessity of keeping the size and weight of their rucksacks to a manageable limit. The following check-list will cover the requirements of most trekkers following any of the routes described in this book.

Rucksack (day-sack only for members of an organised group trek)

Kitbag (for group trekkers only; these fit onto a porter's doko)

Boots (lightweight boots are best; also spare laces & cleaning kit)

Light shoes (trainers preferred)

Socks (outer and inner, to your own requirement)

Trousers/breeches (light cotton for travel, hotel-use and on trek; plus a thicker pair for colder conditions);

Long, loose skirt for women.

Shirts (1 for travel/Kathmandu; 2 or 3 for trek use)

Sweater (or fibre-pile jacket)

Down jacket

Cagoule & overtrousers

Underwear (include thermal-wear for cold conditions)

Sleeping bag (4 seasons plus; also sleeping bag liner)

Insulation mat (Karrimat or similar)

Gloves (thermal inner & warm outer mitts)

Balaclava (or woollen hat)

Sunhat & sunglasses

Water bottle (1 litre capacity)

Headtorch (plus spare bulbs and batteries)

Mending kit

Toilet kit (inc. 2 small towels)

Toilet paper (& lighter to burn same if caught out on trek)

First aid kit

Whistle	Map & compass
Plastic bags	Guidebook
Penknife	Notebook & pens
Small padlock (to secure kitbag for group trekkers, or to lock bedroom for those staying in lodges)	Camera & films (also spare batteries and lens tissues)
	Passport (& spare passport photos)

It is good to have a complete change of clothing waiting for your return from trek, and most Kathmandu hotels have a storage facility. Make sure your left luggage is secure and clearly marked with your name and expected date of return.

MAPS

The World is a country which nobody ever yet knew by description; one must travel through it one's self to be acquainted with it.
(Lord Chesterfield)

So it is with trekking in the Annapurna Himal, for the available maps, though perfectly adequate for day-to-day travel on the clear, well-trodden trails, do not properly suggest the wonders of these mountains, nor indeed, give a true indication of the topography. Not only are contours (where shown) somewhat approximate and at times confusing, certain villages have been marked on the wrong side of a river, some not shown at all, while a single tea-house may be depicted in letters as large as those reserved for some villages. Altitudes vary from sheet to sheet, spellings differ too.

But none of this really matters. The important thing to remember when orienting yourself in Nepal, is the name of the next village along your trail. Simply ask directions from the first person you meet, and off you go. If the maps do not match the standard of those you're used to at home, see that as an advantage; confusion only adds to the adventure.

Several maps have been published for the Annapurna region; those most readily available and adequate for trekking purposes are the following:

Round Annapurna Himal (at a scale of 1:225,000) published by Mandala
    Graphic Art. Covers the whole area included in this guidebook,

except Dumre, and has descriptive text on reverse.

Pokhara to Jomsom Manang (1:125,000 scale) published by Mandala Trekking Maps. A dyeline relief map without contours. In the series "Latest Trekking Map" - also covers all the region described in the present book.

Annapurna Conservation Area (1:125,000) published by ACAP. A contour map with major trekking routes marked; informative text printed on the reverse.

GETTING THERE

The farther one travels, the less one knows. (Chinese saying)

By Air:

There are eight international airlines that fly to Nepal, and those linking Europe with Tribhuvan International Airport, Kathmandu, include the following:

Royal Nepal Airlines Corporation (RNAC), Biman Bangladesh Airlines, Pakistan International Airlines (PIA), and Lufthansa.

Royal Nepal have twice-weekly flights from London, calling at Frankfurt and Dubai. They become heavily booked well in advance of the main trekking seasons, so think ahead if you hope to travel with them. Royal Nepal will also arrange charter flights on request.

Flights by Biman and PIA necessitate connections in Dhaka and Karachi respectively. Lufthansa flies direct from Frankfurt to Kathmandu.

Other flights can be arranged that require connections via India, but be warned that the bureaucracy involved in organising transit at Delhi Airport can be somewhat tedious.

Flights out of Kathmandu are always completely booked during the main trekking seasons. It is essential to reconfirm homeward flights at least 72 hours before departure time. Failure to do so may lead to the loss of your seat and you will then have plenty of time to regret the omission. Before spending all your Nepalese currency, check the amount of departure tax to be paid at the airport.

By Other Means:

Trekkers heading for Nepal from India will find that a combination of rail and road travel will take about three days for the journey from Delhi to Kathmandu by way of Agra, Varanasi, Patna and the border crossing at Birganj, near Raxaul. The most convenient road crossing for a direct journey to be made to Pokhara is the border at Sonauli, near Bhairawa. Buses link Bhairawa with Pokhara. Coming from Darjeeling it is possible to take an Indian train to Siliguri, and taxi from there to the border post at Kakar Bhitta which has buses to Biratnagar in eastern Nepal. Buses and RNAC planes ply the journey from Biratnagar to Kathmandu.

Entering by road from Tibet is by way of Kodari, but this crossing is often closed by landslide during the monsoon.

All vehicles entering Nepal must have an international *carnet de passage*.

Travel Within Nepal:

Domestic flights are operated by RNAC and one or two other independent airlines, and all flights by foreigners must be paid for in U.S. dollars. Of particular interest to trekkers in the Annapurna region is the regular scheduled service from Kathmandu to Pokhara. Bookings for this flight are made at the International Reservations Office of RNAC on New Road, Kathmandu. Other flight opportunities within the Annapurna region centre on the STOL airstrips at Jomosom in the Kali Gandaki and Hongde (Manang) in the Marsyangdi. But like all remote STOL flights, delays must be expected since weather conditions need to be settled; too many clouds in Nepal conceal mountains. In Kathmandu reservations for domestic flights (other than those to Pokhara) by RNAC are made at the office in Thapathali.

Buses daily ply the 200 kilometres (125 miles) of bumpy road between Kathmandu and Pokhara in anything from nine hours upwards - depending on the number of breakdowns. Public buses used by locals offer cheap "entertaining" travel, but these can be desperately uncomfortable and will leave you in need of a good rest before beginning your trek. Slightly less uncomfortable tourist overland buses are run by agents with offices in Thamel. These are only a little more expensive than public buses, and the difference will be worth paying. Public buses start their journeys from the bus terminal near Ratna Park, or from the bus station by the Central Post Office. Those run mainly for tourists leave from the Central

Immigration Office around 7.00am. Reservations should be made at least a day in advance. Booking agents in Thamel display large signs advertising this service outside their offices.

Those planning to trek the Annapurna Circuit, beginning at Dumre some two hours short of Pokhara, will still have to pay the full Pokhara fare. When your rucksack is being loaded onto the roof of the bus in Kathmandu, make a point of telling the packer that your destination is Dumre and not Pokhara. It will then be easier to locate on arrival.

Buses stop at several tea-houses along the road for refreshment, at various police check-posts and, usually, at Mugling for lunch. Make sure you eat as soon as possible after stopping, and don't wander far from your vehicle as the driver is likely to set off without too much formality once he is ready. This is not the time to become separated from your baggage.

NEPAL - FACTS AND FIGURES

There can be no other country so rich in mountains as Nepal.
(H.W.Tilman)

Rectangular in shape and measuring roughly 800 kilometres by 240 (500 miles x 150), Nepal contains the largest collection of 8000 metre (26,000ft) peaks in the world. But mountains form only the northern part of this beautiful country. In the south is the tropical belt of the Terai - an extension of the Gangetic plain - while the broad central region is one of fertile hills rising from 600 to 2000 metres (2000-6500ft) in altitude. The sub-tropical Kathmandu valley is included in this central strip, as are neighbouring valley basins.

It is the world's only Hindu monarchy. Officially some 90% of the population of about 18 million are said to be Hindu and just 8% of the Buddhist faith, but Hinduism and Buddhism merge compatably in so many different ways here that it is not always easy to separate them. When trekking in the Annapurna region one sees more evidence of Buddhism than of any other faith, and since Buddhists are much more tolerant of outsiders than are Hindus, one has several opportunities to visit monasteries and to photograph symbols of their faith along the way.

The official language, Nepali, is derived from Pahori which comes from northern India and is spoken by some 58% of the population. But it has been said that there are as many different languages in Nepal as there are races, and as many dialects as there are villages. In the Kathmandu valley the original language is Newari, which uses no less than three different alphabets. Fortunately for the Western trekker English is widely understood in Kathmandu and in most lodges along the popular trails, and most Sherpas who generally make up the crew of organised treks also speak a modicum of English - while the more educated among them often learn smatterings of other European languages too.

Although it numbers among the six poorest nations on earth in terms of per capita income, the trekker in Nepal does not experience the same sense of hopeless poverty that is so prevalent in a number of other Eastern countries. For by far the majority of its population depend for their livelihood on agriculture, much of which is subsistence farming on the intricate terraced fields that create such an artistic picture on the hillsides. Some 17% of land is under cultivation, and about 30% covered by forest. However, while Nepal was self-sufficient in food production in the early 1950s, the demands of a fast-growing population and corresponding increase in livestock, has seen that self-sufficiency fade to one of grain-deficiency and a rapid reduction in forests. Nepal now faces serious economic and environmental problems which only considered development can arrest.

Tourism is the largest source of income (only 2% of labour is employed in industry), and trekking provides much-needed foreign currency essential to the country's development, although at present Nepal relies very heavily on foreign aid programmes for major development projects - some of which may be questionable in the light of the problems outlined above.

International telecommunication is possible through the British earth satellite station, installed in 1982. Telephone connections with Europe and the United States are good, and are generally available from Kathmandu and Pokhara. A number of offices and hotels now have fax facilities.

Nepalese time is 5 hours 45 minutes ahead of Greenwich Mean Time (15 minutes ahead of Indian Standard Time; 13 hours 45 minutes ahead of San Francisco).

Postal services are dealt with in Kathmandu at the General Post Office located at the junction of Kantipath and Kicha-Pokhari Road. The office is open daily (except Saturdays and public holidays) from 10.00am to 5.00pm (4.00pm November to February). Always ensure that stamps on postcards, letters or parcels are franked by the counter clerk at the time of posting. There is always a queue at the special counter in the Post Office reserved for franking stamps. Several villages on the trails round Annapurna have Post Offices of some description. Postcards and letters may be sent from these, but again make sure that stamps are franked at the time of posting.

Nepalese currency is the Rupee (Rps) which is made up of 100 Paisa. It is a "soft" currency and cannot be taken in or out of the country. Travellers cheques and "hard" currency can be exchanged at Tribhuvan Airport, Kathmandu, and at a number of banks which are open daily (except Saturday) from 10.00am until about 2.00pm. Always collect your exchange receipts as these will be needed when applying for trekking permits and visa extensions. It is important to collect plenty of small-denomination notes for use on trek almost as soon as you arrive in Nepal. It is no good stopping at a wayside tea-house a week's walk from the nearest bank and expect to pay for your cup of tea with a Rps 500 or Rps 1000 note.

TIME IN KATHMANDU

And the wildest dreams of Kew are the facts of Kathmandu.
(Rudyard Kipling)

Kathmandu is one of the world's most magical capital cities and it is worth devoting a few days, either before or after trek, to absorbing its unique atmosphere and exploring neighbouring towns within the valley. After weeks in the mountains it is a great place to sample a change of menu too, for there are dozens of restaurants to satisfy all appetites. There are numerous hotels and guest-houses of varying degrees of comfort, and enough shops and street traders offering a thousand and one "bargains" to help you spend the last of your money.

Kathmandu is a kaleidoscope of colour, of smells, of noise. There

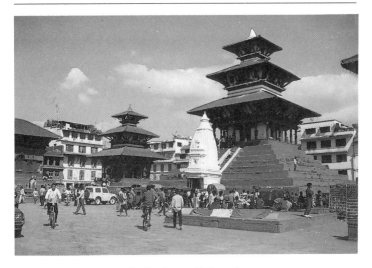

Durbar Square, Kathmandu

are people everywhere. The narrow alleyways and broad modern streets are all thronging with activity. Traffic streams in an endless honking procession through the daylight hours along the main highways. Bicycle rickshaws and taxis bounce and weave through the narrow lanes of Thamel, somehow managing to avoid colliding with the crowds of traders, the bustle of porters, tourists and beggars, and the occasional cow.

Thamel, the ever-popular district in the north-west of the city, has a plentiful supply of budget accommodation in small hotels and guest-houses, a fine selection of restaurants, as well as bookshops, suppliers of climbing and trekking equipment, outfitters of all kinds, and a specialist trekker's food shop. You could spend days here alone.

But it is the wealth of religious and cultural sites that makes Kathmandu so extraordinarily appealing. "There are nearly as many temples as houses, and as many idols as inhabitants," wrote W.Kirkpatrick in 1811, and while there are certainly more houses and inhabitants today, plus great numbers of tourists, there is no shortage of places to visit. The following suggestions merely scratch the

43

KATHMANDU

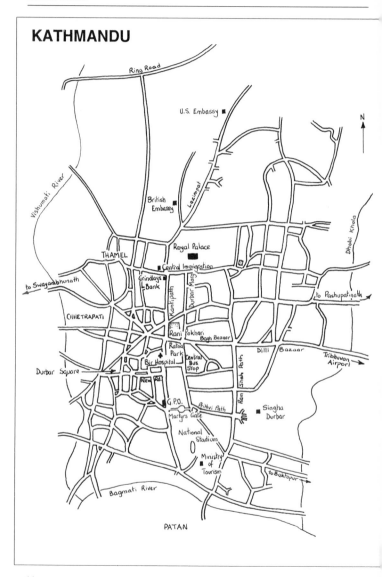

surface, but for more detailed information, background history and as a pointer to the full glories of the valley itself, readers are directed to the *Insight Guide: Nepal* (APA Publications) which is highly recommended.

Kathmandu:

Durbar Square is a must. Dominated by the great Taleju Temple it contains more than fifty important monuments, shrines and temples as well as the Hanuman Dhoka (the Royal Palace), and offers a superb roofscape of exotic shapes. Intricate wooden carvings adorn every building: figures, faces, patterns and religious symbols by the metre on struts and beams, and around doorways and windows. Early morning is the best time to visit. Street vendors are setting out their wares, porters gather to await employment, the faithful scurry to various temples for their first devotions of the day, and the place comes alive with streams of light, colour and movement. By mid-morning the Square is crowded.

North-east of the city Bodhnath's dome, 40 metres high (130ft), makes it the largest Buddhist stupa in all Nepal. Seen from afar it is recognised as the country's centre of Tibetan culture. Monasteries and pilgrim rest-houses cluster around, and at the start of the Tibetan New Year lamas take part in colourful ceremonies here. Masked dances are performed for the public in a nearby field, while other dances take place in a monastery courtyard.

On a site considered sacred more than 2500 years ago, the great *stupa* of Swayambhunath looks down on Kathmandu from its hilltop perch to the west of the city. A long flight of steps leads to it among trees around which monkeys play, and from the top of it a grand view looks out over the valley. A row of prayer wheels encircles the *stupa*, and behind it there's a *gompa*, or monastery, which visitors are free to enter. Inside hundreds of butter lamps flicker, while the sounds of drums, gongs and trumpets accompany each devotion.

The Vishnumati river flows between Kathmandu and Swayambhunath, while the Bagmati twists round the eastern side of town and is bordered by Pashupatinath, the largest Hindu shrine in Nepal. The Bagmati is a tributary of the Ganges and is considered sacred by Hindus. Overlooking it is a temple complex whose entrance is forbidden to non-Hindus, but on the east bank a series of terraces provide viewpoints from which to study not only the gilded temple opposite, but also riverside activities below. In the river women do their laundry; others take part in ritual bathing, while Hindus fast approaching death are lain on stone slabs with their feet in the water until all life has drained from them. Nearby ghats are used by commoners for cremation, and at other times for celebration. Other ghats are reserved for the use of royalty.

Patan:

South of Kathmandu, and divided from it only by the Bagmati river, Patan is a very old city indeed. Some claim that it was founded in the third century BC by the Buddhist emperor Ashoka and his daughter Carumati. Primarily a Buddhist town it has around 150 former monasteries, but there are also many Hindu temples and shrines and scores of exotic buildings, so that it would take months of study to properly visit each one.

This "town of a thousand golden roofs" has its own Durbar Square with the one-time Royal Palace facing a complex variety of Newari architectural wonders. The Palace itself has three main courtyards open to the public, each displaying the skills of woodcarvers of past generations. Nearby the beautiful Kva Bahal, or Golden Temple, dates from the twelfth century.

Like Kathmandu, Patan is a bustling town but with a vibrancy all its own. When you've absorbed as much spiritual and architectural wonder as you can, stroll among the bazaars and enjoy haggling with the street vendors for bargains.

Bhaktapur:

Also known by its former name of Bhadgaon, this handsome town of about 50,000 lies 16kms (10 miles) to the east of Kathmandu. Badly damaged in 1934 by the same earthquake that so devastated the capital, it nevertheless retains much of its medieval character and is in many respects the finest town in the valley to visit for its architectural delights. Much of the restoration work has been made possible through a German-Nepalese development project that has so far helped preserve some 200 buildings without destroying their essential character. The route to Bhaktapur from Kathmandu is a pleasant one, for it travels through open country and then climbs among pine trees and alongside two small reservoirs on the outskirts of the town itself.

Durbar Square here is entered through a gateway, and at once you are confronted with a spacious approach to a collection of temples and monuments. At least two large temples were completely destroyed by the earthquake, but those that remain are set out with sufficient space to enable the visitor to study them from different angles without their being confused among other crowding buildings.

Whilst Durbar Square is the main focus of attention in Bhaktapur, a short stroll leads to Dattatraya Square in the Tachupal quarter of town with its fifteenth-century temple and lively atmosphere, and Taumadhi Square in the centre of town, surrounded by lovely old Newari houses. Both are worth exploring, as are the many narrow alleyways. Take particular note of the magnificent carvings that adorn so many buildings, especially around the windows and doorways. The art of woodcarving here has reached the very height of perfection.

THE ANNAPURNA CIRCUIT

In such country there is no monotony. (H.W.Tilman)

Widely acknowledged as one of the world's classic treks this tremendous route makes a long horseshoe loop of the Annapurna Himal. Preferably tackled in an anti-clockwise direction to give a somewhat less-demanding approach to the Thorong La than would be required from the west, the trek links the valley of the Marsyangdi Khola with that of the Kali Gandaki. The Thorong La (5415m: 17,766ft) is the lynch-pin of the route; if conditions are unfavourable for its crossing the circuit cannot be completed.

Whilst the trail along the Kali Gandaki had been an important trade route for centuries, probably the first Westerner to see it was the Swiss geologist, Arnold Heim, who flew through the valley in 1949 in a Dakota and brought back some unique photographs of the mountains. The following year members of the successful French expedition to Annapurna I, under the leadership of Maurice Herzog, explored the Kali Gandaki and made their base at Tukuche. By remarkable coincidence, at the very same time Bill Tilman was leading a small party through the Marsyangdi to Manang, from which they made an attempt on Annapurna IV. (Tilman's party included Jimmy Roberts, who later explored the Annapurna Sanctuary and who was to become the "father" of trekking in Nepal when he established his Kathmandu-based company, Mountain Travel, in 1965.) Gaston Rebuffet was possibly the first European to cross the Thorong La during the French expedition's reconnaissance, whilst a few days earlier he, along with Herzog and Marcel Ichac, had traversed the Tilicho La which also links the two valleys.

By the 1960s a combination of political difficulties, mainly stirred by the Chinese invasion and occupation of Tibet, effectively put the region out of bounds to foreign visitors. But in 1977 the Nepalese Government at last lifted restrictions on the Manang valley, and for the first time the Annapurna Circuit became a reality for adventurous trekkers.

The route begins in either Dumre or Gorkha: the first being on the Kathmandu-Pokhara highway with the Marsyangdi flowing from the north; the second (Gorkha) being accessible from the same highway by a side road. From Dumre a dirt road strikes north along the Marsyangdi to the village of Besisahar, a saving of about two days of walking. From Gorkha an alternative trail crosses a ridge and continues to Tarkughat in the Marsyangdi, mid-way between Dumre and Besisahar: a two-day prelude. A third option is to take a series of seldom-trekked trails across-country from Sisuwa, south-east of Pokhara, to Khudi in the Marsyangdi. Superb views along this route include most of the snow-capped peaks from Annapurna to Manaslu: a three-day trek.

The trail through the Marsyangdi valley is always clear on the ground, although confusion might arise at one or two minor path junctions where there are no obvious indicators as to which alternative is the one to take. Whilst the ACAP authorities have erected a few signposts indicating the route to Manang, there will be no other signs or waymarks - in this alone the Himalayan trekking experience proves to be very different from that of European mountain regions.

There are dozens of villages on the Circuit, and even more tea-houses spread along the trail. Lodges are in plentiful supply and there are lots of good campsites for organised parties. Mountain and valley views are constantly changing and are never less than magnificent. The initial stages wind among rich terraces of vegetation, but soon give way to the savagery of the Marsyangdi's gorge. This in turn leads to the stark landscapes of the Manang valley in the rain-shadow of the mountains.

The route crosses and re-crosses the river countless times. Most of the suspension bridges are sturdy and with good handrails on both sides, which is comforting when you see (and hear) the river furiously thrashing through its bed below.

On reaching Manang it is advisable to spend a couple of days there to aid acclimatisation, then take two short days to walk up to Thorong Phedi in preparation for the 985m (3200ft) ascent to the pass. In clear conditions and with no snow lying, the only difficulties experienced in crossing are caused by the altitude, and in the actual distance from Phedi to Muktinath on the far side. In snow, or with poor visibility or a strong wind blowing, the Thorong La gives a very

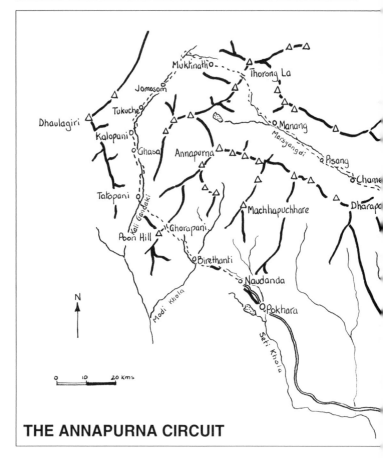

THE ANNAPURNA CIRCUIT

demanding day. At no time should the potential seriousness of its crossing be undervalued. It is essential that all members of the party, including porters, have clothing adequate to cope with sub-zero temperatures on the approach to the pass.

From Muktinath the route descends easily to the bed of the Kali Gandaki and then works its way south between Dhaulagiri and the Annapurnas, through countryside which contrasts markedly with

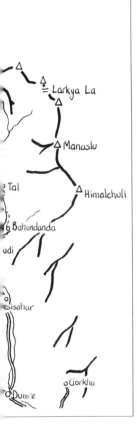

that experienced on the eastern side of the Thorong La. Lodges are as numerous as in the Marsyangdi, but of a higher standard.

Below Tatopani the trail leaves the Kali Gandaki's valley and begins a relentless climb among lush vegetation to the Poon Hill Danda where outstanding views are to be had of the big mountains through whose gateway you have recently passed. Beyond Ghorapani two or three more days of walking are required to reach Pokhara, while those with sufficient time and energy can add a few days to their trek by breaking away from the Poon Hill Danda to visit the Annapurna Sanctuary.

The route is written in fifteen stages, but it is important to add to these acclimatisation days in Manang (two recommended) and at least one rest day in the Kali Gandaki valley. On top of these you may well feel it worth reducing some of the longer stages described in order to spend more time in certain villages, or to stray into side valleys to explore further. At the very minimum you should allow eighteen days for the circuit, but where possible make more available in case your crossing of the Thorong La is delayed by bad weather. The Annapurna Circuit is generally considered a three-week trek.

ROUTE PROFILE:
ANNAPURNA CIRCUIT (BESISAHAR - MUKTINATH)

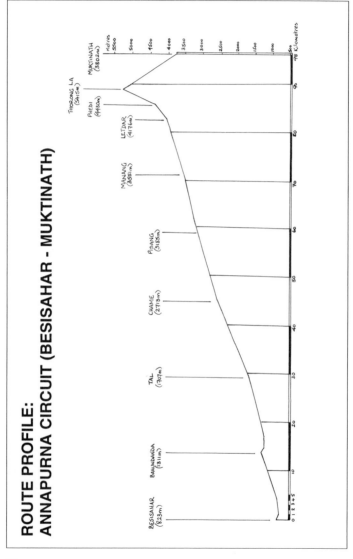

BESISAHAR (823m)
BAHUNDANDA (1311m)
TAL (1707m)
CHAME (2713m)
PISANG (3185m)
MANANG (3551m)
LETDAR (4176m)
PHEDI (4480m)
THORONG LA (5415m)
MUKTINATH (3802m)

PROLOGUE STAGE 1:
KATHMANDU - DUMRE - BESISAHAR

Distance:	**175 kilometres (110 miles)**
Time:	**1-2 days**
Accommodation:	**Lodges in Dumre, Bhote Odar,**
	Phalenksangu and Besisahar.
Transport options:	**Bus (Kathmandu to Dumre)**
	Truck or jeep (Dumre to Besisahar)

Under normal circumstances it is quite feasible to leave Kathmandu in the morning and arrive in Besisahar the same evening, ready to begin the trek proper the following day. By virtue of the road being pushed into the valley of the Marsyangdi, this motorised prologue has become the most popular approach. Of course, it is always possible to trek along the dirt road from Dumre to Besisahar (a two-day option) but there is little pleasure in sharing the track with occasional smoke-belching, dust-cloud raising vehicles. Better to get to Besisahar as soon as possible and begin the walk from there. First, though, the ride from Kathmandu to Dumre.

As mentioned in the introductory chapters, public buses depart Kathmandu every morning bound for Pokhara. Tourist "express" buses leave from outside the Central Immigration Office around 7.00am. Seat reservations are essential; tickets may be obtained at least a day in advance from various agents whose boards advertise this service in Thamel. Although you will be leaving the bus at Dumre, about two hours short of Pokhara, you must pay the full Pokhara fare. (It is still remarkably cheap.) Baggage is carried on the roof. When passing your rucksack to the man loading it, make a point of telling him that your destination is Dumre, rather than Pokhara.

Buses depart from Kathmandu in a noisy caravan of blaring horns. It can be an exciting journey: first along the Kathmandu valley, then over the Chandragiri Pass on a ridge that forms a rim to it, before winding down into a new valley system. The road descends to the banks of the Trisuli River - a rafter's delight - and bumps on along a road built with Chinese aid. It is regularly disturbed by landslips and the heavy monsoon rains, and at various points along the way traffic is held up while essential repair work is being undertaken.

The journey from Kathmandu to Dumre can take anything upward of five hours. There are one or two halts for refreshment, but these do not always have adequate toilet facilities. At **MUGLING** (about 110kms: 68 miles from Kathmandu) buses usually make a lunch stop. You are advised not to stray too far from your vehicle. Prospective trekkers have been known to find themselves stranded in the town while the bus carrying their luggage trundles off in a cloud of dust and smoke.

DUMRE (440m: 1444ft) is a busy place whose main street is lined with shops and lodges run by Newars, the original inhabitants of the Kathmandu valley. Porters begin their journeys to far-distant villages from here, taking weighty supplies on their backs along the well-padded trails of the middle hills.

Open-backed trucks ply the 40kms (25 miles) of rough dirt road between Dumre and Besisahar, leaving town as soon as they are full - which means about fifty trekkers crammed uncomfortably aboard and unable to sit. It is a very cheap way to travel. It is also an unbelievably dusty, bone-shaking ride of about five hours. An alternative is to hire a jeep. This offers a faster ride, and with the certainty of a seat, but is considerably more expensive than the truck ride - you should agree a price before leaving Dumre. As for discomfort, there can be little to choose between the two means of conveyance. Both are virtually guaranteed to leave their passengers in Besisahar dirty, shaken and with crashing headaches - and longing for the peace and beauty of the winding trail. Keep your trek permit handy, as there are at least two check-posts along the track to Besisahar.

BESISAHAR (823m: 2700ft) is a large village and the administration centre of Lamjung District. There are several trekkers' lodges, an assortment of shops, police check post, post office and hospital. It should be possible to hire porters or a porter-guide here for the journey ahead, if required.

Manaslu Himal from the foothills west of Khudi

STAGE 2:
BESISAHAR - KHUDI - BAHUNDANDA

Distance:	**14 kilometres (9 miles)**
Time:	**6-7 hours**
Start altitude:	**823m (2700ft)**
High point:	**Bahundanda 1311m (4301ft)**
Height gain:	**488m (1601ft)**
Accommodation:	**Lodges in Khudi, Bhulbhule, Ngadi and Bahundanda**

The first day's walk should be taken steadily. With more than two weeks of trekking ahead you'll need to adapt to the rhythm of the trail; slip into a comfortable stride and absorb the whole experience of this magical land. There will be patches of sub-tropical forest along the way, terraces of agriculture stepping the hillsides, lush vegetation typical of the middle hills of central Nepal, insect-seething trees, and views upvalley to Himalchuli, Peak 29 (Ngadi Chuli) and Manaslu, the world's eighth highest mountain.

There will be rivers to cross and recross by way of suspension bridges and, above Bhulbhule, the first of many delightful, slender waterfalls spraying down the valley walls.

A number of small villages lie on today's route. These are peopled by Brahmins, Chhetris, Gurungs or Manangbas. Traditionally, Brahmins are the Hindu priest caste and Chhetris the warrior caste, while Gurungs have their own religious practices that can be either Hindu or Buddhist. Gurungs are noted shepherds, peasant farmers or Gurkha soldiers; they make up the majority of the population in the Annapurna region and are found mostly in the middle range of hills where a number have recently made a successful transition to businessmen. In Bhulbhule a few Manangba (the people of the Manang valley) have responded to the increasing number of visitors and have moved down from the arid upper valley to operate trekkers' lodges.

There are two routes upvalley as far as Bhulbhule; one on either side of the Marsyangdi. The trail on the east side is reached by a bridge that crosses from Besisahar; it goes by way of Simalchaur and will take almost three hours to reach Bhulbhule. The main trail, however, is that which follows the west bank and is described below.

Wander through Besisahar heading north (upvalley) and at the far end of the village continue by descending into a narrow tributary valley. Halfway down the slope there is a small settlement with a pipal tree at a trail junction. Take the right fork and soon after cross the side stream to climb steeply at first on the far side, then contour round a hillside spur alongside subtropical forest and cultivated terraces, and come to a small village of orange-walled houses.

The trail passes the village and slants down towards the Marsyangdi, hills on either side of the valley being heavily vegetated, and about two hours from Besisahar you will come to the Bhoran Khola, a river draining the western hills. There is no bridge, but a series of stepping stones make it possible to cross without getting wet feet, if the water level is low. After heavy rain crossing could be tricky. Just beyond the river sit the few buildings of **SERA** *(refreshments)*.

About 30 minutes later the path enters a grove of trees with another cluster of houses *(refreshments)*, and soon after brings you to the Khudi Khola, a substantial river flowing down from the north. Across this river is seen the village of **KHUDI** (792m: 2598ft 2hrs 45mins *accommodation, refreshments*). To get to it there are two suspension bridges about 10 minutes apart; the second being the most recent. Khudi is a small Gurung village near the junction of the Khudi Khola and the Marsyangdi whose houses are roofed with either thatch or tin. Apart from one or two lodges and tea-houses, it also has a few shops. (An alternative trail climbs above the west bank of the Khudi Khola to reach the Gurung village of Ghanpokhara high on the ridge to the south of Telbrung Danda.)

The Annapurna Circuit trail rises among the village houses of Khudi before easing round to the right above the Marsyangdi. Views ahead now include Ngadi Chuli and Himalchuli, both of which received their first ascents from Japanese expeditions. The route continues without difficulty and about 45 minutes from Khudi comes to another suspension bridge, a long one this time over the Marsyangdi, across which is seen **BHULBHULE** (846m: 2776ft $3^1/_2$hrs *accommodation, refreshments*). Accommodation and refreshments are available on both sides of the bridge. The literal translation of Bhulbhule is "the place where water springs from the ground"; this spring is found not far from the path.

Through Bhulbhule continue upvalley among more low terraced fields, with the big snow mountains teasing far ahead, and pass below a lovely thin ribbon of a cascade. Just beyond it the trail forks. Unless the river is high it is possible to take either path for they converge a little later.

About 30 minutes from Bhulbhule pass through another small village with tea-houses where once again the trail divides. Take the left fork and in a further 30 minutes come to **NGADI** (930m: 3051ft $4^1/_2$hrs *accommodation, refreshments*). This small village, set among terraces, is divided by a side stream. The street is paved and lined with lodges and shops. Above it two valleys converge, and in 10 minutes you will come to a small settlement and a suspension bridge across the Ngadi Khola. Cross the bridge and follow the path heading up the left-hand valley, that of the Marsyangdi. It gives the appearance of being somewhat wild, but its steep eastern side has been substantially worked and the trail begins a long climb towards Bahundanda, nearly 400 metres (1300ft) above. It's a fine trail, climbing among the terraced fields and passing attractive groups of houses, some offering accommodation. Bahundanda is seen on its ridgetop overlooking the agricultural corrie through which you climb, and is reached about $1^1/_2$ hours from Ngadi bridge.

BAHUNDANDA (1311m: 4301ft) is perched on a saddle in a narrow ridge of hills, a spur of the Nagi Lekh. It boasts a school and a few lodges and shops. There is a police check post beside the trail to the left of the main square, and fine views to the north. It is the last Brahmin village in the Marsyangdi valley; its name actually means "Brahmin hill".

STAGE 3:
BAHUNDANDA - SYANGE - TAL

Distance:	16 kilometres (10 miles)	
Time:	$6-6^1/_2$ hours	
Start altitude:	1311m (4301ft) (5600ft)	*High point:* **Tal 1707m**
Height gain:	396m (1299ft)	
Accommodation:	**Lodges in Syange, Jagat, Chamje and Tal**	

This stage of the trek leads into the first of the Marsyangdi's gorges, gorges which will dominate much of the journey between Bahundanda and the upper valley near Pisang. But it's not all dark defiles trapped in shadow, for there are broad open areas too where views are long and challenging, and sunny stretches where terraced fields of millet, rice or barley ripen to add palettes of colour to the scene.

On this stage the landscape changes dramatically. There's also a change in vegetation, with forests of rhododendron and pine, with marijuana growing beside the trail and, towards Tal, a high altitude pastureland as an indication of advancing height. Another indication of increased elevation is felt towards darkness when a chill sets in - so different from the soft warmth of the lower country. And, finally, there is a difference in the inhabitants of the upper villages visited on the way to Tal. Now a distinct Tibetan influence is apparent in the features and clothing of the villagers, and the first hint of Buddhist culture too. That will be an integral part of the walk for many days to come.

North of Bahundanda the trail descends steeply, winding through a magnificent curve of rice or millet terraces, their patterns artistically set and the morning light soft upon them. The Marsyangdi curls far below. Crossing a side stream the way then makes a long traverse of the right-hand hillside, undulating easily among the terraces. When you look back it is to gain a clear impression of the natural amphitheatre through which you have just descended, and of the brief gorge carved by the river to the west of Bahundanda's hill spur. Despite the steepness of the terrain terraces have been created in the most impossible situations, turning the hillsides into vast stairways.

The trail leads through few settlements and past only an occasional tea-house. Several more side streams are crossed and vistas remain fine along the valley ahead. After 1$^{1}/_{2}$ hours the path edges a large flat shelf of hillside and passes a solitary lodge *(accommodation, refreshments)*. This is Hotel Waterflow - which currently advertises a massage service - and just beyond it begins a steep descent towards the river. On the opposite side of the valley an attractive waterfall crashes in long ribbons of spray.

Cross to the west bank of the Marsyangdi over a suspension bridge and enter the village of **SYANGE** (1136m: 3727ft 1hr 45mins *accommodation, refreshments*). Hotels and tea-houses line this one-street village, and beyond it the Marsyangdi narrows to a gorge. The continuing trail heads up valley, climbing and falling as a switchback, and about half an hour from Syange comes to a tea-house/lodge standing alone on the hillside. A long and steep climb follows among marijuana growing wild beside the path, and with overhanging rocks in places. At the top of one particularly steep rise stands a small, solitary tea-house. Ahead you can see the next village of Jagat, and the path to it eases round the hillside high above the river - fortunately this has improved considerably since Tilman's visit in 1950. Then he found slender wooden galleries fixed across the face of the hill, but the galleries, he said, "were pretty frail, particularly the hand-rails which were better left alone or at the most touched rather than grasped".

JAGAT (1314m: 4311ft 3hrs 15mins *accommodation, refreshments*) apparently used to be a customs post set in a forest clearing in the days of the salt trade with Tibet that thrived for centuries until 1959 when, in the wake of the Chinese invasion, cross-border trade with Tibet ended. A few lodges and tea-houses have helped enlarge the village now, and offer refreshment on the way through; bananas grow among the surrounding trees.

The way beyond Jagat continues to descend and in 10 minutes a sign indicates that 4 minutes further down the hillside towards the river there are hot springs and a lodge providing *refreshments* and *accommodation*.

The trail now levels out and begins to climb once again through lush forest, emerges to another level section to pass opposite more fine waterfalls, and then comes to **CHAMJE** (1433m: 4701ft 4hrs 15mins *accommodation, refreshments*). Ahead the valley is squeezed into another gorge, even more narrow and dramatic than before.

Descend from Chamje and go across the river by way of a suspension bridge, and then wind up the hillside among huge boulders, passing opposite yet another waterfall and entering the Marsyangdi's continuing gorge. The climb becomes quite steep in places. About 45 minutes from Chamje you will reach another small tea-house. Beyond this you lose a little height before climbing again to another tea-house enjoying superb views downvalley through the deep river-cut narrows. Continue uphill a short distance and, topping a rise, suddenly before you lies an open, flat pastureland. The Marsyangdi winds in lazy curls below, soft blue and gentle. Ahead lies Tal nestling in the pastures, big mountains soaring on either side to dwarf the village into a collection of toy houses. It is very much a Shangri-La view.

The path eases down to the pastures, rims the right-hand side of the valley and, nearing the village, you see a classic waterfall bursting out of the mountainside behind it.

TAL (1707m: 5600ft) occupies the site of a silted-up lake (the name of the village means 'lake') formed when a landslide blocked the gorge. It is a strange place with a unique atmosphere; the most southerly village of Manang district it is inhabited by a number of people of Tibetan origin, and the Buddhist influence is clearly evident. The main street is wide and lined with several lodges and shops. Horses are often to be seen either tethered outside the lodges or roaming the street unattended. Behind the village there is plenty of space for camping.

STAGE 4:

TAL - DHARAPANI - CHAME

Distance:	**15 kilometres (9¹/₂ miles)**
Time:	**6¹/₂-7 hours**
Start altitude:	**1707m (5600ft)**
High point:	**Chame 2713m (8901ft)**
Height gain:	**1006m (3301ft)**
Accommodation:	**Lodges in Dharapani, Bagarchhap, Dhanagyu, Lattemarang and Chame**

A grand day's journey through ever-varied landscapes, in addition to the basic height difference of more than 1000 metres there's plenty of switchbacks on the trail to add to the total elevation gain. There's more gorge walking to be had, but you also enter an alpine-style region with the fragrance of pine, and snowpeaks growing ahead. Views are of Manaslu again, and of Lamjung and Annapurna II as the valley curves westward above Dharapani.

At the entrance to a number of villages now the trail passes through a stone kani, *or entrance* chorten. *Some of these are decorated inside with Buddhist paintings. There will be mani walls and lines of prayer wheels, and you should remember always to pass along the left-hand side of these. In Bagarchhap there is a gompa worth visiting for its frescoes.*

At Dhanagyu, upvalley from Bagarchhap, an alternative trail climbs to the south to the high pastures and camping ground of Timung Meadows. It then crosses the pass of Namun Bhanjang before descending to the main trail near Kodo. This strenuous route, rewarded by some spectacular views, was for a long time the normal way for much of the year to reach the Manang valley from the south. The main trail used today, however, is much less demanding but was created only with the help of dynamite and a lot of physical effort.

North of Tal the Marsyangdi's gorge closes the valley again with a deep U-shaped cleft. Leaving the village the trail passes a small, low-roofed watermill set beside a stream, and soon after you enter the steep-walled gorge again. In 30 minutes from Tal the trail forks. Take the left-hand option to skirt the base of some cliffs, then cross the Marsyangdi on a wooden bridge and continue upvalley now on the west bank. About 20 minutes later the way climbs past a small settlement with a few tea-houses, and continues high above the river on a well-made traversing path before descending again to the few houses of **ORAD** (1880m: 6168ft 1hr 15mins *refreshments*). This small village is in two sections about 15 minutes apart. Both have tea-houses. Just beyond the lower half cross the river again, this time on a long suspension bridge. On the east bank stands the white-walled Hotel Dorchester, and 5 minutes from it there is a meagre hot spring.

The trail continues upvalley, gently undulating above the river for another 25 minutes. You then descend a number of steps and recross the Marsyangdi yet again by another suspension bridge. Five minutes later enter **DHARAPANI** (1943m: 6375ft 2hrs *accommodation, refreshments*). This is a pleasant village near the confluence of the Marsyangdi and Dudh Khola. Dharapani has a police check post beside the trail, reached about 10 minutes after entering the first part of the village.

On the opposite bank of the river, where the valley forks, you can see the village of Thonje. From it a trail winds through the valley of the Dudh Khola to cross the (1) Larkya La, a 5213 metre (17,103ft) pass which gives access to the north side of Manaslu and to the Buri Gandaki, a route which Tilman's party explored in 1950.

Our trail ignores both Thonje and the Dudh Khola, bears westward and now enters a more alpine-type region on the north side of the Lamjung Himal. Climbing among fragrant pine trees and with good views back through the Dudh Khola, the way heads over a spur and, half an hour from Dharapani, goes through a Buddhist *kani* and enters **BAGARCHHAP** (2164m: 7100ft 2¹/₂hrs *accommodation, refreshments*). This is an attractive and interesting village of flat-roofed stone houses, many of which are stacked high with firewood. There are several solid-looking lodges and tea-houses, and partial views ahead to Lamjung and Annapurna II; the first climbed in 1974 by a British expedition, the second by Chris Bonington, Dick Grant and Ang Nyima as part of an expedition led by Jimmy Roberts in 1960. With its *gompa* and prayer flags Bagarchhap is very much a Buddhist village; the way out takes you past a wall of prayer wheels and between drystone walls, and you should give a moment to look back at views of (2) Manaslu now to the east.

The continuing route ignores a bridge just outside the village, and remains on the left of the river all the way to Chame. It heads among forests of blue pine and in 45 minutes from Bagarchhap comes to the small settlement of **DHANAGYU** (2290m: 7513ft 3hrs 15mins *accommodation, refreshments*) amid walled, stony pastures and with fine views again back to Manaslu.

Now heading into another gorge the way climbs again, crosses a side stream which drains the glaciers of the Lamjung Himal, and thereafter steadily rises through forest with the Marsyangdi thundering steeply below. A bridge of stone and concrete is crossed beside an impressive waterfall (another tributary stream coming from Lamjung Himal); then you climb a staircase of stone, at the top of which the trail levels before descending to another small settlement about 1hr 45mins from Bagarchhap.

Climbing again the path winds among forests of rhododendron, oak and maple and comes to the collection of Tibetan-style houses of **LATTEMARANG** (2454m: 8051ft 5hrs *accommodation, refreshments*). Continue on the switchback trail, sometimes beside the river, sometimes high above it. Yet another wooden bridge crosses a side stream, then up in zig-zags towards a hillside spur, which is turned to the right, and pass the Karma Hotel *(accommodation, refreshments)*, a solitary building set upon the hillside.

Impressive rock scenery rises ahead; great faces soar above the river and are topped with pines. At last you emerge from the forest to a clearing and enter the village of **KODO** (2629m: 8626ft 6hrs *accommodation, refreshments*), a two-part village of flat-roofed houses and lodges, separated by a 10-minute walk. The second part of the village is more substantial than the first and has a police check post. From the village you can see Annapurnas II and IV. The rarely-trodden tributary valley of (3) Nar-Phu can be seen to the north.

The final half-hour walk is mostly along a broad and easy trail led by drystone walls, at the end of which lies **CHAME** (2713m: 8901ft). Chame is the administrative centre for the Manang district and as such is a bustling place with a number of trekkers' lodges, shops and even a bank. The town has electricity, a police check post and post office. Overlooking it is the beautiful peak of Annapurna II which is particularly fine with the early morning sun on its upper snowfields.

Points of Interest Along the Way:

1: THE LARKYA LA (5213m: 17,103ft) at the head of the Dudh Khola gives access to the valley of the Buri Gandaki, thus making possible a circuit of Manaslu, Peak 29 and Himalchuli. This circuit, matching the Annapurna Circuit in length, is usually begun in Gorkha and, like that of the present route, is tackled in an anti-clockwise direction, descending through the Dudh Khola to Thonje and then reversing the route already described from Dharapani to Dumre, or across-country to Pokhara from Khudi. At present only self-contained trekking parties are officially allowed into the Buri Gandaki region accompanied by a liaison officer.

2: MANASLU (8163m: 26,781ft) is a beautiful ice peak, the world's eighth highest, that was studied by Tilman during his 1950 approach march to the north side of Annapurna. It became the focus of a succession of Japanese expeditions in the ensuing years. During one of these local villagers effectively stopped the attempt on religious grounds, but the summit was eventually reached from the Larkya Glacier by Imanishi, Gyaltsen Norbu, Kato and Higeta, members of an expedition led by Yuko Maki in 1956.

3: NAR-PHU is the name given to the tributary valley seen from Kodo. It is a splendid "hidden" valley guarded by steep walls of rock which leads between Pisang Peak and Kang Guru, and is one of the three districts of Manang. Until recently Nar-Phu enjoyed almost total seclusion from Western influence. There are only two villages in the valley with a total population of about 850, and although a number of trails lead into its upper reaches, for many years it was out-of-bounds to foreigners. For an insight into the valley, see Windsor Chorlton's *Cloud-Dwellers of the Himalayas*.

STAGE 5:

CHAME - BHRATANG - PISANG

Distance:	**13 kilometres (8 miles)**
Time:	**4 hours**
Start altitude:	**2713m (8901ft)**
High point:	**Pisang 3185m (10,449ft)**

Annapurna III (7555m) (Circuit. Stage 6)

Winter conditions between Manang and Letdar (Circuit. Stage 7)

Annapurna massif from the trail to Thorong Pedri (Circuit. Stage 8)
Descending to Muktinath, Dhaulagiri in the background (Circuit. Stage 9)

| *Height gain:* | 472m (1548ft) |
| *Accommodation:* | Lodges in Taleku, Bhratang, Pisang and Upper Pisang |

Above Dharapani the Marsyangdi carves a trench below the northern flanks of the Annapurna-Lamjung massifs. Walking upvalley, as we are, is to enter the rain-shadow of the Himalaya, and it is on today's stage that the effects of this rain-shadow become evident. Whilst at Chame there is still sufficient vegetation to bear witness to an overflow of the monsoon. The area is alpine, but still wooded. But as you approach Pisang, and having finally emerged from the Marsyangdi's gorge, all this begins to change. The landscape becomes more arid and the first evidence of wind erosion leaves its signature on the valley rather more boldly than does that of rain.

This is a short, but delightful stage. The only villages between Chame and Pisang are Taleku and the Khampa settlement of Bhratang, now resited on the east bank of the river. In addition to these two small communities there are a few tea-houses to provide welcome refreshment along the way.

Almost immediately upon leaving Chame the trail crosses to the north bank of the river and soon begins to climb among pinewoods. Between the trees lovely views are to be had across the valley to the soaring peaks and ice-crests of the Annapurnas, 5000 metres (16,000ft) above the river. In a little under 45 minutes you come to **TALEKU** (2804m: 9199ft 45mins *accommodation, refreshments*), a small village with one or two lodges.

The route now establishes the pattern for the day: alpine-like the trail switchbacks up and down, often through pine forest above or beside the river. There is a landslide area to cross, but then the way continues as before - and always with rewarding views.

An hour from Taleku you enter an open, level area of scattered pine and walled orchards of low-growing apple trees leading to the village of **BHRATANG** (2919m: 9577ft 1hr 45mins *accommodation, refreshments*), an interesting Tibetan-style village with prayer flags flapping in the breeze and a long mani wall at the entrance. Maps show Bhratang as being on the west side of the river. Indeed, this is where it used to be, but in 1975 the Tibetan warrior refugees (*Khampa*) who formerly lived there, were resettled. Parts of the old village remain, while this "new" village serves trekkers who no longer need

Less than two hours from Chame you come to Bhratang, a Tibetan village

to use the trail on the opposite bank since a new path has been blasted in the walls of the gorge ahead.

Keep on the east bank and 15 minutes beyond Bhratang the trail cuts through the steep rock face that walls a section of the gorge. Half an hour beyond this you will come to a suspension bridge with another seen a short distance upstream. Overlooking the valley now is the vast, impressive slab face of Paungda Danda, a huge sheet of curving rock scraped clean of vegetation and towering more than 1500 metres (5000ft) above the Marsyangdi.

Cross the bridge and climb a series of steep zig-zags into forest. It's a wearisome stretch, but the shade of the pines will be welcome on warm days. For some time the forest trail leads on, passing a rather basic tea-house on the way, and about three hours from Chame you emerge to a view overlooking the Manang valley, here known as Nyesyang; a lovely flat-bottomed, broad and arid valley, but with stunted pines and low-growing juniper everywhere and (1) Pisang Peak rising to the north. There's a chorten clustered with prayer flags and a solitary tea-house here, **POKHARI DANDA** (3185m: 10,449ft 3hrs *refreshments*). Just below lies a small reedy tarn, the "pokhari" from which the tea-house gains its name.

The continuing trail keeps to the left of the tarn and heads gently through the valley, clear and mostly level. This is without doubt a region denied much of the benefit of monsoon rains. Rain clouds from the south are deflected by the big mountains of the Annapurna Himal, and the valley makes a fair imitation of parts of Tibet. The Marsyangdi continues to flow through, but it is not the full-bodied river seen lower down, and it writhes through a twist of carved brown soil.

Soon the dun-coloured houses of Upper Pisang can be seen like swallows' nests on the hillside ahead. Keeping to the left of the river in an easy hour from Pokhari Danda you come to **PISANG** (3185m: 10,449ft). This is a spartan village set in a barren land. There are several lodges to accommodate trekkers and those who use the village as a base from which to tackle Pisang Peak which rises behind the upper village and whose summit cone of snow and ice can easily be seen from the valley. At the western end of lower Pisang there is a large square with a long mani wall with inset prayer wheels. Above the river water is diverted through wooden conduits to power two small mills. Far ahead can be seen the snow-capped Chulu East around whose lower slopes the trail wanders from Manang to the Thorong La.

UPPER PISANG (3292m: 10,801ft) is reached in 20 minutes from the riverside village. It is an amazing place with a medieval air, and every building has its wand of prayer flags. It too has lodge accommodation. From it a magnificent view encompasses the valley through which you've been walking, but most dramatic of all, it gazes directly at the shapely peak of Annapurna II walling the valley to the south. Even if you decide to stay in lower Pisang, a visit to the upper village is highly recommended.

Points of Interest Along the Way:

1: PISANG PEAK (6091m: 19,984ft) rises high above the village after which it is named, but is severely foreshortened from this point. The graceful pyramid that forms its upper reaches is better seen from above Hongde. It is one of the "trekking peaks" accessible from the valley - others are Chulu East and Chulu West above Manang - and it was first climbed in 1955 by a member of a German expedition bound for Annapurna. Views to Annapurna II are magnificent from the upper slopes. For detailed route information see Bill O'Connor's *The Trekking Peaks of Nepal.*

STAGE 6:
PISANG - HONGDE - MANANG

Distance:	**13 kilometres (8 miles)**
Time:	**4 hours**
Start altitude:	**3185m (10,449ft)**
High point:	**Manang 3551m (11,650ft)**
Height gain:	**366m (1201ft)**
Accommodation:	**Lodges in Hongde, Braga and Manang**

There are two route options for the trek between Pisang and Manang; the first is the main valley route described below. The second is a longer, more strenuous high route which visits two medieval villages perched way above the valley on the northern hillsides; this is given as Alternative Stage 6. Both routes are interesting and visually delightful.

The following stage is the standard route which provides a short and undemanding walk. It leads through the broadening valley with little in the way of height gain, while the mountains of the Annapurna Himal grow in stature as a great southern wall. At Hongde there is a STOL airstrip operating scheduled flights to Pokhara and, occasionally, to Kathmandu. It is used mainly by the local Manangba who, contrary to appearances, have established a reputation for being sophisticated world-travellers who regularly make business trips to the capital cities of Asia. For two centuries the Manangba have enjoyed special trading privileges, a fact which Tilman noted in his 1950 visit when he commented upon their "strikingly independent ways and their manners". He also reported, rather laconically: "We found no wireless sets in Manangbhot, but a man whom we attempted to photograph retorted by whipping out a camera himself."

At Braga a centuries-old gompa is worth a visit, but since it is advisable to spend at least one full day (but preferably two) based in Manang in order to acclimatise before tackling the Thorong La, it might be worth leaving the gompa to be visited during this acclimatisation period.

At various points along the trail there are Buddhist symbols that

Pisang peak - a 'trekking peak' - seen above Hongde

underline the religious practices of the valley: chortens, prayer wheels, prayer flags, mani walls and kanis. The Manangba are more closely related to the people of Tibet than they are to the Nepalese of the middle hills; they have similar features, customs, manners and dress, and practice a form of Tibetan Buddhism. And even the countryside in these upper reaches of the

Marsyangdi has a scenic affinity with that of Tibet to the north, as opposed to the lower section of the valley with its lush vegetation.

Follow the well-trodden trail out of Pisang heading upvalley. It soon begins to climb a short but steep wooded spur that descends from Annapurna II effectively squeezing the valley. From the ridge of this spur the fascinating, broad upper Manang valley is spread out before you in all its wind-eroded glory: a strangely sculpted semi-desert with Tilicho Peak (7134m: 23,406ft) rising nearly 30kms (19 miles) away as part of a great enclosing wall.

Descend from the spur into the flat bed of the valley and come to **HONGDE** (3322m: 10,899ft 1¹/₂hrs *accommodation, refreshments*). Also known as Ongre, this is an important village on account of the STOL airstrip and police check post situated there. It's not a particularly attractive place, though, and has just one broad main street whose finest feature is a long mani wall down the centre. Several lodges line the street and boast the innovation of electric lighting from a hydroelectric station.

Walk through Hongde, but make sure you have your trekking permit checked at the police post situated at the western end of the village - the last opportunity to do so until you reach Muktinath. Beyond the village the broad trail crosses a tributary stream and grants superb views into the amphitheatre created by the curving ridges of (1) Annapurnas III and IV. Just to the right of the trail nestles a small tarn; fine views from here show Pisang Peak behind you to the east.

Again the long wall of peaks grows in stature along the southern flank of the valley, while Chulu East and Chulu West (both trekking peaks over 6000 metres - 19,600ft) hog the northern slopes. Tilicho Peak draws you on. It's a splendid walk and so easy underfoot that you can forget the trail and simply amble along enjoying the views.

Near the few buildings of **MUNGJI** (3482m: 11,424ft 3hrs) the trail crosses the Marsyangdi for the very last time on a sturdy wooden bridge, and half an hour later reaches **BRAGA** (3505m: 11,499ft 3¹/₂hrs *accommodation, refreshments*), a collection of houses built in tiers against a steep, eroded cliff-face whose upper crags form turrets, pinnacles and organ pipes of rock above a white-painted *gompa*. A string of electricity wires sagging between crazy-angled poles makes an incongruous addition to the scene.

The way continues in the floor of the valley, breaks across some fields, goes over a stream by a watermill and up a narrow trail to pass through a white *kani* on a hillock guarding the entrance to **MANANG** (3551m: 11,650ft), the main village of the upper valley. There are, of course, plenty of lodges here.

For further details, see the section headed Time In Manang which follows Alternative Stage 6.

Points of Interest Along the Way:

1: ANNAPURNAS III and IV are linked by an extensive ridge that was first reached by Tilman's party in 1950 on their attempt to climb Annapurna IV. Annapurna IV (7525m: 24,688ft) is the easternmost summit of the two, a near neighbour to the more difficult and higher Annapurna II, and it received its first ascent from a German expedition just five years after Tilman was beaten back. Annapurna III (7555m: 24,787ft), on the other hand, was not climbed until 1961 when an Indian expedition put three men on top. From its summit a long ridge system extends southwards. This is seen in all its glory from the Sanctuary; a beautiful ice-fluted crest that projects over the peak of Ghandharba Chuli (also known as Gabelhorn) and up to Machhapuchhare.

ALTERNATIVE STAGE 6:

PISANG - GHYARU - NGAWAL - MANANG

Distance:	**15 kilometres (9 miles)**
Time:	**5¹/₂-6 hours**
Start altitude:	**3185m (10,449ft)**
High point:	**Ghyaru 3673m (12,051ft)**
Height gain:	**488m (1602ft)**
Accommodation:	**Lodges in Upper Pisang, Braga and Manang**

This is the high route option on the way to Manang, a fairly strenuous option too - much more so than the modest amount of height-gain would suggest. But the rewards are tremendous. From Upper Pisang and the trail leading from it there are wonderful views to enjoy. Both Ghyaru and Ngawal are fascinating villages in their own right, and vistas from them - and from the path which links them - are quite stunning. Be warned, though, that the path heading up to Ghyaru is the steepest of the route so far and will surely tax all but the fittest of trekkers - especially those who are carrying full rucksacks. It will be a good test of your standard of fitness before tackling the Thorong La.

Leave Pisang, cross the Marsyangdi by way of a wooden bridge near the western end of the village and take the path which climbs through fields to **UPPER PISANG** (3292m: 10,801ft 20mins *accommodation, refreshments*). Annapurna II appears majestic above the flat-roofed houses which, with their long strips of prayer flags, provide a photogenic foreground. (There is another path which veers left across the Marsyangdi, avoids Upper Pisang and joins the described trail a short way upvalley.) From the upper village the trail makes an easy traverse of hillside heading north-west, goes through patches of pine and juniper and above a small green tarn. It then descends into a pine-speckled basin in which there is a long mani wall. Shortly after this the trail crosses a side stream flowing from Pisang Peak and then divides. Take the upper path which now climbs steeply in numerous zig-zags, and as it does, so views are shown ahead to the curious eroded cliffs that threaten to block the Marsyangdi way below.

It is a demanding ascent, but eventually you come onto a shelf of hillside at the village of **GHYARU** (3673m: 12,051ft 2hrs), an astonishing medieval collection of stone-built houses, the stones simply laid one on top of another in a sometimes rather ad-hoc fashion. Typically, one house appears to stand upon the jutting roof of the house below. Prayer flags slap against upright poles from almost every rooftop, and views across the valley to the northern wall of the Annapurnas are again spectacular. There do not appear to be either tea-houses or lodges in Ghyaru, although trekkers may possibly be invited into local homes for refreshment.

Narrow alleyways twist through the village and pass a mani wall. Just outside Ghyaru the continuing trail takes you past a water-driven prayer wheel and a number of chortens. At first leading between stony fields outlined with drystone walls, it then becomes a fine belvedere of a path offering superb views all the way.

Rounding a long jutting hillside spur you come into view of the next village set across a broad shallow slope with the Manang valley beyond. Gangapurna, Tarke Kang (Glacier Dome) and Tilicho Peak look magnificent upvalley. Passing through another *kani* enter **NGAWAL** (3650m: 11,975ft 3hrs *refreshments*), a larger village than is Ghyaru and with more opportunities for the cultivation of a basic agriculture in the fields surrounding it.

Leave the village by cutting down into a shallow scoop of a valley on a clear trail that loses much height, then slants off to the right into the bed of the main Marsyangdi not far from the Hongde airstrip. (Should you require refreshment at this point it is advisable to cross the river to Hongde where there are lodges, and join the main trail to Manang from there.)

Remain on the northern side of the river and continue along the path to round a band of cliffs, beyond which you join the main trail by the few buildings of **MUNGJI** (3482m: 11,424ft 4$^{1}/_{2}$hrs). Manang is about an hour's walk upvalley.

TIME IN MANANG

Above Manang there are no more large villages; indeed, apart from Tengi, half an hour's walk upvalley, there are no permanent settlements until you reach Muktinath on the western side of the Thorong La. The Thorong La is almost 2000 metres (6500ft) higher than Manang and having reached an altitude of 3551 metres (11,650ft) already it is important now to allow time to acclimatise before proceeding further. One or two days at least should be set aside for acclimatisation and Manang makes a good base for this. It also provides a last opportunity to hire a porter-guide for the crossing, if required. Enquire at one of the lodges for a reliable man.

The village is typical of the upper valley in its architecture and in its Tibetan influence. The houses are stone-built with flat roofs reached by log "ladders" whose rungs are little more than cupped notches cut out of a sawn tree trunk. A maze of narrow alleys lead among the houses, opening here and there to a square with a wall of prayer wheels and teasing views of the mountains opposite. There's no shortage of lodges or camping places. There are plenty of shops that stock food supplies and numerous assorted goods, including gloves, socks and sunglasses, for inadequately equipped porters. There's a post office and a medical post run by the Himalayan Rescue Association. In the latter, each afternoon during the main trekking seasons, one of the volunteer doctors on duty gives a lecture on altitude sickness. This lecture is highly recommended, and none but the most experienced of high mountain trekkers should miss the opportunity to listen in and to note the clear message given.

From Manang you gaze across the valley to a wonderful array of high mountains. Gangapurna (7454m: 24,455ft), first climbed by a German expedition in 1965, has a glacier hanging down its northern flanks. Below it lies trapped a small icy lake. Annapurna III is to the east of Gangapurna, and beyond that the long ridge which extends from it to Annapurna IV. West of Gangapurna is Tarke Kang (7193m: 23,599ft), which was formerly known as Glacier Dome, and Tilicho Peak (7134m: 23,406ft) stands well to the north-west of that. Below Tilicho Peak, but unseen from Manang, lies Tilicho Lake which was discovered by Maurice Herzog in 1950 when he and other members of his French expedition were searching for Annapurna. On that occasion he had crossed the Tilicho La from Tukuche in the valley of the Kali Gandaki and descended to Manang where he hoped to buy provisions. But Manang seemed then a very poor village with nothing to spare and he returned to Tilicho Lake empty handed.

It seems strange, when Manang is now so obviously geared to trekkers, that in 1950 there was practically no spare food to be had at all there. Tilman had a similar experience to Herzog, although he at least managed to base himself in the village for some time. He found the Manangba to be inhospitable; they were reluctant to sell food to their visitors or to provide porters for them, but Tilman deduced that their winter trading ventures abroad probably brought them sufficiently lucrative rewards that money offered by the Europeans provided no real incentive for them to change their ways. Happily a very different experience will be had by today's trekkers in Manang.

Whilst using the village for acclimatisation purposes there are several interesting features in the area worth visiting. The first is the centuries-old *gompa* downvalley at **BRAGA**. Variously quoted as being 500 or even 900 years old, it is certainly the oldest monastery in the valley, and it contains numerous manuscripts, a large Buddha, rows of terracotta statues, butter lamps and thankas. In the upper building there's a collection of ancient knives, swords and home-made muskets. The *gompa* is described by David Snellgrove in his book, *Himalayan Pilgrimage*. Although normally kept locked, the guardian has an uncanny sixth-sense that lets him know when anyone wants to visit. He appears from nowhere, keys jangling, to show you around. Another *gompa* in the vicinity is **BODZO**, which is found high on a ridge between Braga and Manang.

Opposite Manang the small lake trapped below the icefall of the Gangapurna glacier makes a short but interesting excursion. The village of **KHANGSAR**, on the route to Tilicho Lake west of Manang, may also be visited on an acclimatisation day walk, but Tilicho Lake itself is too far away to get there and back in less than two or three days, and for those who wish to visit this magical place below the Great Barrier, it will be necessary to take camping equipment and food.

The crossing of Tilicho La, however tempting the prospect might be, may not be practical, since military exercises are regularly held on the west side of the pass and apparently some trekkers are known to have been turned back by the army and forced to return over the pass to Manang. Another group of trekkers was trapped at the lake for over a week by heavy snowfall in October 1985, and three sherpas lost their lives there.

The ridge above Manang to the north provides more spectacular views, while an easy half-hour's walk up the trail to **TENGI** is also worth considering. From this village you gain a rewarding overview of the valley and of the great wall of the Annapurna Himal stretching as far as the eye can see off to the south-east. Tengi, of course, is on the route to the Thorong La.

STAGE 7:

MANANG - LETDAR

Distance:	10 kilometres (6 miles)
Time:	4 hours
Start altitude:	3551m (11,650ft)
High point:	Letdar 4176m (13,701ft)
Height gain:	625m (2051ft)
Accommodation:	Lodges in Tengi, Gunsang, Yak Kharka and Letdar

Above Manang the valley forks. The left branch is sliced by the Khansar Khola which drains the Tilicho Lake region. At its head is Tilicho Peak and the ice wall of the Great Barrier, so-named by Herzog. The right-hand branch, heading north-west, leads to the Thorong La and is walled on the east by Gundang, Chulu East and Chulu West. This latter valley, the valley of the Jhargeng Khola, is a narrow one with steeply plunging hillsides. In places the mountains seem to gather round in a close embrace; they tower overhead and protect much of the route through from the cold winds. In snow, with clear skies and no wind, daytime temperatures can be very warm; but nights are bitterly cold.

As part of the important acclimatisation programme it is advisable to take two days for the walk from Manang to Thorong Phedi, base for the crossing of the Thorong La. In order to achieve this steady altitude gain, the rather basic lodges of Letdar offer overnight accommodation and meals for "tea-house" trekkers, while there is plenty of level ground nearby to provide camping space for organised parties with tents.

It may be a short walk to Letdar (also spelt as Lattar or Leder), but it is a visually spectacular route with wonderful views to the Great Barrier, Gangapurna and Annapurna III. It is a steady climb and never too steep for comfort, although those who are slow to acclimatise will feel it is demanding enough for one day.

The lodges at Letdar offer very basic, limited facilities. In the main trekking season bed-space fills quickly; it is therefore important not to arrive too late in the day. Having said that, accommodation on the Annapurna Circuit is constantly growing and improving, so we may confidently expect an upgrading of Letdar in the not-too-distant future.

Chorten on the trail above Tengi

Take the trail out of Manang and head up valley, winding between terraced fields to reach the village of **TENGI** (3642m: 11,949ft 30mins *accommodation, refreshments*). From Tengi there is a splendid view back down to Manang, and across to Gangapurna's icefall. The trail skirts round the left-hand side of the village and on the outskirts passes a long mani wall adorned with a row of worn prayer wheels and prayer flags.

The trail soon begins to curve north-westward into the tributary valley of the Jhargeng Khola, the stream which joins the Khangsar Khola to form the Marsyangdi. Across to the west note the position and shape of Tilicho Peak. On the walk down to Jomosom from Muktinath the north side of this fine mountain will be in view.

Climbing again you come to a wayside chorten from which there are more grand views downvalley. The route continues and about 1¹/₂ hours from Manang passes a solitary tea-house. A few minutes later reach the small settlement of **GUNSANG** (3879m: 12,726ft 1hr 40mins *accommodation, refreshments*) and, continuing, soon pass another lodge.

There are few steep ascents to contend with and height is gained without too much effort. Whilst the mountains ahead lack the charisma of the Annapurna massif behind, the whole scene retains a wild kind of beauty, while the backward view is never less than magnificent. **YAK KHARKA** (3968m: 13,018ft 3hrs *accommodation, refreshments*) consists of a couple of *goths* (temporary shelters) about five minutes apart, the second of which provides overnight lodging and meals. Above the mountains squeeze the valley; (1) Chulu West rises high overhead while the western line of peaks conceals any hint of a possible route over.

Beyond Yak Kharka the trail rises round the right-hand hillside, crosses broad yak pastures (look out for *bharal* - the blue sheep - which are sometimes seen nearby), then descends into a gully to cross a side stream on a wooden bridge. The climb out on the far side is rather steep, but once over the rise, a little over an hour from Yak Kharka, you come to the first of two rough lodges at **LETDAR** (4176m: 13,701ft). The second of these is reached by a short stroll along the trail. Although it is an austere place Letdar enjoys a superb high mountain view out to the south-west.

Points of Interest Along the Way:

1: CHULU WEST, with its neighbour, Chulu East, is on the list of available trekking peaks. (The Round Annapurna trekking map mistakenly reverses the position of these two peaks, while other summits in the same massif are not marked at all.) Despite confusion it would appear that Chulu West received its first ascent at the hands of a Japanese expedition as early as 1952. This, and others in the group, has been climbed many times since and makes a popular ascent by a choice of routes. A base camp is usually set by climbing expeditions in a high valley approached from the Thorong La trail.

STAGE 8:

LETDAR - THORONG PHEDI

Distance:	**5 kilometres (3 miles)**
Time:	**1¹/₂-2 hours**
Start altitude:	**4176m (13,701ft)**
High point:	**Thorong Phedi 4430m (14,534ft)**
Height gain:	**254m (833ft)**
Accommodation:	**Lodge at Thorong Phedi**

It might be tempting to add this very short stage to the previous day's walk, but at these altitudes it is sensible to achieve height gradually. Often those who trek from Manang to Phedi in one day have time to regret it and spend an additional day in Phedi trying to cope with a bad headache and feelings of nausea. It is said that villagers from Manang think nothing of riding from their village to Muktinath in just one day - what their horses think of this is not recorded. But for trekkers trying to cope with problems of altitude, a more gradual approach is advisable.

Except under a fresh fall of snow the trail continues to be clear and well-defined. There are one or two sections where it is a little exposed, and others where the gradient is steeper than you might wish. But overall it's not a difficult walk. There are no refreshment facilities along the way.

Phedi means "foot of the hill" and really refers to the meadowland at the end of the valley; plenty of camping space is available there. Lodge accommodation, however, is found 10-15 minutes above, on the trail to the pass, and 10 minutes above that there is another possible camping area. The

The basic lodge at Letdar

quality of the water remains highly suspect. Accommodation, however, is much better than its reputation, as is the meals service. The staff do a fine job in very difficult circumstances, catering for large numbers of (sometimes) demanding trekkers in an extremely remote position. Anyone familiar with the mountain hut system in the European Alps will be content with what is offered at Phedi, but to those who jibe at crowded dormitories and the sometimes slow production of meals, I would say: have patience, consider the problems faced by those who staff the lodge, and above all, retain your sense of humour. The experience of Phedi can, and should, be a positive one. Note that, contrary to the lodge system in operation elsewhere on the Circuit, at Thorong Phedi you pay for your bed upon arrival, and meals as you receive them.

From Letdar the trail winds upvalley at a comfortable gradient high above the river, but then climbs steeply for a short way. After this an easy traverse is followed before you descend to the river and a wooden bridge. About an hour from Letdar cross the bridge. As the valley here has narrowed to a tight V the subsequent climb up the western slope is rather steep and tiring. But this is fortunately short-lived and is followed by a long traverse. The path is narrow and a little exposed in places. It leads across screes, then enters a broad meadowland with a low stone building set upon it. Backing the meadows huge cliffs, reminiscent of the Dolomites, sweep round in an amphitheatre to block the valley. This is **PHEDI (4404m: 14,449ft 1¹/₂hrs)**.

The continuing trail skirts the left-hand side of the meadow, zig-zags up the hillside and about 15 minutes later comes to the lodge buildings of **THORONG PHEDI** (4430m: 14,534ft). Set upon a natural shelf below a steep hillside cone are several low, single-storey stone buildings that provide accommodation for more than 100. In the wake of bad weather a backlog of trekkers builds up to stretch facilities to the limit. The staff work all day to produce a constant supply of food and drinks; there is also a small store on the premises that sells bottled drinks, biscuits etc. It is important to sign in and pay for your bed as soon as you arrive. And don't forget to drink plenty of liquids at this altitude.

STAGE 9:
THORONG PHEDI - THORONG LA-MUKTINATH

Distance:	12 kilometres (7¹/₂ miles)
Time:	6-12 hours
Start altitude:	4430m (14,534ft)
High point:	Thorong La 5415m (17,766ft)
Height gain:	985m (3232ft)
Descent: 1613m (5292ft)	
Accommodation:	Lodges in Muktinath (possibility of beds at Chatar Puk 1hr above Muktinath)

Crossing the Thorong La is the high point, in every respect, of the Annapurna Circuit, and it represents the single major difficulty to be faced. Trekkers who have not acclimatised sufficiently will find the crossing a misery. In snowy conditions it becomes a serious proposition; cold, high winds and the advanced altitude together ensure that it is not undertaken lightly. Although trekkers are known to have made the journey in unusually mild, snowless conditions wearing shorts and trainers, no-one should contemplate setting out on the trek without adequate clothing and equipment to cope with extremes of cold. Frostbitten toes and fingers, and even fatalities among ill-equipped trekkers and their porters occur most years. The Thorong La is more than 600 metres (1900ft) higher than the summit of Mont Blanc, highest mountain in the European Alps. Bear that in mind and you'll get its crossing in perspective.

There are more spectacular mountain passes in this world than the Thorong La, it is true, yet this one is rather special in that it is very much the lynch-pin on which completion of the route depends. The ascent, in settled conditions, is arduous only on account of the altitude, but it takes you into the very heartland of the high mountains; a heartland of great beauty that ought to be absorbed as you trek ever upward. From the pass a new landscape begins to unfold, and the descent to Muktinath will gradually reveal the glories of the valley walk to come, as Dhaulagiri signals the way with its pure and graceful cone of ice shining like a beacon in the sun.

Invariably there will be trekkers at Phedi determined to set out at the unearthly hour of 3.00am - or even earlier. This is not only unnecessary, but could be dangerous on account of the extreme cold generally experienced before dawn. Being exposed to such temperatures for hours at a time without a warming breakfast can quickly lead to hypothermia. Make a point of setting out about an hour only before dawn. The staff at the lodge begin to serve breakfasts about 1½ hours before sunrise, thereby enabling you to get away in good time and with some food and warm drink to fortify you.

The steepest part of the ascent is experienced at the very beginning, as you set out from Thorong Phedi. The trail climbs in long zig-zags up the left-hand side of the scree cone above the lodge buildings. Generations of shepherds and cross-border traders have used this route for centuries, so the trail, though narrow in places, is clear in snowless conditions. In a little over an hour it brings you through a cleft, or minor pass, at the top of the steep cone from which lovely views can be enjoyed. This is the first of many false cols, and having crossed through the trail now veers leftwards, soon to enter a secretive inner mountain region.

Traversing steep slopes, climbing rocky ridges and moraines the trail continues to work a way upwards. The first stream from which you can fill water bottles is reached about 1½ hours from Thorong Phedi. (Remember to treat the water with iodine.) A second source is located about 30 minutes later.

Although there are so many false cols, do not despair, but appreciate the magnificent high mountain views which are a special feature of this part of the trek. Try to enjoy the whole experience. When weariness weighs you down consider that as being just one aspect of the price you pay for being gifted with the opportunity to take part in this epic journey. As you gain height towards the pass use your rest stops to absorb the grandeur of the scene out to the south where, after spending so many days in its close company, the Annapurna range is about to disappear from your field of vision.

The pass is seen nearly half an hour before you come to it, and is reached by a broad, gentle slope. Ahead the giant cairn with its cluster of wind-tattered prayer flags that marks the summit beckons you on. Depending upon trail conditions, individual fitness and degree of acclimatisation, the **THORONG LA** (5415m: 17,766ft) is reached in anything from three to six hours.

Above to the south rises the proud, glaciated peak of Khatung Kang (6484m: 21,273ft); to the north Yakawa Kang (or Thorungtse 6482m: 21,266ft) sometimes shows itself to be a snowfree rock peak. Behind, the Chulu peaks make a splendid wall of ice and snow. But ahead to the west the countryside appears barren, a dun-coloured vertical desert dusted with snow. Far below lies the Kali Gandaki (otherwise known as the Thak Khola). Crossing the Thorong La you pass from one world to another; although it is no true watershed it effectively separates two contrasting landscapes. And as you descend towards Muktinath those contrasts become increasingly evident.

The descent is long and as tiring as the ascent, a knee-jarring effort that will take between three and six hours to walk from Thorong La to Muktinath. From the pass the trail veers left and then goes down the centre of the valley, winding to and fro along what appears to be a central spur of moraine. Care is sometimes required to avoid losing the path; when covered with snow it is often extremely slippery and can prove treacherous; without snow it is dusty and also inclined to be slippery. It takes you down a number of moraine spurs, and as you lose height so Dhaulagiri grows in stature far off.

At the foot of the moraines you reach the first patches of grass and a solitary tea-house, **CHATAR PUK** (c4100m: 13,451ft *refreshments*), which also provides rudimentary accommodation in the main trekking season.

The final descent of about an hour takes you across rough pastures, descends into a narrow gully to cross a stream coming from the left, and then climbs out the other side. Soon after you catch sight of Muktinath on the hillside ahead to the left above the valley of the Jhong Khola. The trail leads directly to it. But first you pass the sacred shrine, revered by both Hindu and Buddhist, which is set among a grove of poplars just off the trail; a walled oasis of reverence. Springs are directed to 108 water spouts shaped like animals' heads around the wall of a Hindu temple, and in a *gompa* a flame from a natural gas jet above a trickle of water is evidence of a miracle: burning water. After Pashupatinath, the shrine at Muktinath is Nepal's most sacred Hindu site. On the walk down to Pokhara it is quite possible that you will pass *sadhus* from far distant Indian cities who have made, or are making, their pilgrimage to this holy place.

MUKTINATH (3802m: 12,474ft) is reached a few minutes beyond the shrine on a streamside path. Officially, Muktinath only refers to the pilgrim site, while the growing settlement below is called Ranipauwa. However, the village is more widely known now to visiting trekkers as Muktinath. It has many lodges, tea-houses, shops and even electricity. Tents spring up in assorted corners of the village, including rooftops. There is a police check post soon after you enter, and a rest house for pilgrims nearby. Sunsets are often quite spectacular from here; Dhaulagiri dominates the vista downvalley while on the northern side of the arid Jhong Khola valley can be seen the ruins of Dzong, at one time the most important village in this part of the mountains and seat of the local ruler. The hillside above it has been savagely eroded by wind, while from the ridgetop it is possible to look down into the basin of Mustang.

ROUTE PROFILE:
ANNAPURNA CIRCUIT (MUKTINATH - POKHARA)

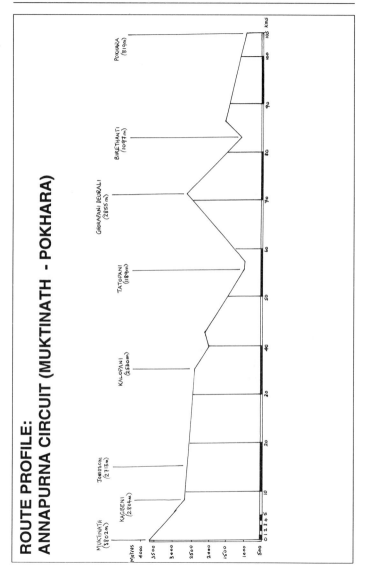

85

STAGE 10:
MUKTINATH - JOMOSOM

Distance:	**15 kilometres (9 miles)**
Time:	**4-4½ hours**
Start altitude:	**3802m (12,474ft)**
Low point:	**Jomosom 2713m (8901ft)**
Descent:	**1089m (3573ft)**
Accommodation:	**Lodges in Jharkot, Kagbeni, Eklebhatti and Jomosom**

After the energetic crossing of the Thorong La a rest day in Muktinath (Ranipauwa) would no doubt be welcome. With a short foray or two into the surrounding countryside there's plenty of interest to fill such a day, while for those a little short of energy there are splendid views downvalley to enjoy while seated upon a lodge rooftop with a cold drink set before you, the life of the village going on below, snow-capped peaks gleaming against a deep blue sky in the distance.

The continuing walk downvalley is full of beauty as you are drawn into that landscape of contrasts that has something of value to study almost every step along the trail. The medieval fortress-like village of Jharkot, a few minutes from Muktinath, makes a striking foreground to a photograph, with the snow-draped north wall of the Kali Gandaki as a backcloth. There are peach trees to contrast the otherwise barren hillsides, irrigation streams and shallow trapped pools to belie the aridity of the Jhong Khola. The Jhong Khola itself long ago carved a deep and narrow gorge, its walls of fluted rock holding numerous small caves that can be seen from the trail. Hillsides far off are yellow, soft-turned ochre, vegetation-free and appearing for all the world like an extension of the Tibetan Plateau; the valley of the Kali Gandaki, known here in its upper reaches as the Thak Khola, is broad and stony, the river that snakes through having begun its life north of the border, well inside Tibet.

In that valley bed it's possible to find strange black stones called shaligrams. *When broken open they reveal fossilised sea creatures, or ammonites, that lived around a hundred million years or so ago in a sea that was lost when the Indian tectonic plate collided with the main landmass of Asia. These* shaligrams, *revered by Hindus for whom they represent several deities, are regularly offered for sale by Tibetan traders at the wayside.*

There are two trails into the Thak Khola from Muktinath and they divide

Arid hillside near the junction of the Jhong Khola and Thak Khola

below Khingar; the right-hand path descends steeply to Kagbeni, while the main trail continues down to skirt a hillside spur with magnificent views to Dhaulagiri and Tukuche Peak before dropping to the two isolated lodges of Eklebhatti where it is joined by the Kagbeni trail. Kagbeni is another medieval village seated at the confluence of the Jhong Khola and Thak Khola. It's a delightful place with a special atmosphere all its own, and is well worth spending an hour or so there. You might even consider stopping for the night, allowing time to explore it properly and to enjoy the incredible scenery displayed from its unique position.

The Jomosom trail wanders through Muktinath heading west and soon reaches **JHARKOT** (3612m: 11,850ft 20mins *accommodation, refreshments*). The path down to this handsome, ancient place first descends to a stand of trees on its western side, then heads along an alley and passes through a *kani*. Just below the village you will come to a major trail junction. Continue straight ahead on the upper path and follow this easily beside streams, drystone walls and trees and then pass along the edge of **KHINGAR** *(refreshments)*.

Below Khingar the hillsides are more arid and barren than ever, but views of Dhaulagiri ahead are magnificent. The Jhong Khola's gorge is off to the right, its strangely sculpted cliffs giving evidence of wind and water erosion that has worked ceaselessly for untold millenia to create a landscape of unique proportions.

Now the way crosses a broad, open scrub plain, high and gently sloping, while to north and west the hills and valleys are tan, featureless and remarkable for the contrasts they offer to the majestic snowpeaks down-valley.

Across this broad plain the trail forks. There are no markers and the junction is not always obvious. The main route continues ahead; the right-hand option descends quite steeply to **KAGBENI** (2804m: 9199ft 2hrs *accommodation, refreshments*), an oasis of a village on the trail leading to long-forbidden (1) Mustang and Tibet. There is a police check post here. The continuing trail to Jomosom follows the bed of the valley down, and in 30 minutes joins the main path at Eklebhatti.

Instead of branching off to Kagbeni, the main trail continues ahead and soon overlooks the flat, stony bed of the (2) Thak Khola (Kali Gandaki). Kagbeni can also be spotted from this main trail. Climbing through a rock band suddenly Tilicho Peak (7134m: 23,406ft), last seen from just above Manang, and Nilgiri North (7061m: 23,166ft) appear ahead, outliers of the Annapurna massif, while on the opposite side of the valley (3) Dhaulagiri (8167m: 26,795ft) appears as magnificent as ever. Between these two monstrous massifs the Kali Gandaki pours its waters through the deepest valley on earth.

The route descends easily to the bed of the valley and reaches the lodge buildings of **EKLEBHATTI** (2758m: 9049ft $2^{1}/_{2}$hrs *accommodation, refreshments*) to be joined by the trail from Kagbeni.

From Eklebhatti to Jomosom the walk continues mostly along the left-hand side of the valley bed, crossing and recrossing numerous rivulets on the way. It's a lovely walk for the views are stunning throughout, but this is a notoriously windy section and it will be a rare day if you can walk through the valley without being battered by the gales that throw sand and grit into your face. The path is not always clear, but you simply keep along the eastern side of the valley, leaving its bed only on a few occasions.

So come to **JOMOSOM** (2713m: 8901ft), the main township of the valley and administrative centre for the Mustang District. Straddling the river it is a large and busy place, the largest habitation on the Circuit by far since leaving Besisahar. It has electricity, lots of lodges, shops, banks, administration buildings, a military post, police check post, a hospital, post office and a STOL airstrip. Scheduled flights link Jomosom with Pokhara, but aircraft only land and take-off from here when weather conditions allow. Once the day's wind picks up, no flights are possible. High above the town soars the shapely Nilgiri North, with Tilicho Peak as its eastern neighbour.

The Thakalis who inhabit the Thak Khola valley are noted hoteliers, and standards of accommodation enjoyed from Jomosom down to Tatopani are likely to be more advanced than those experienced on the route thus far.

Points of Interest Along the Way:

1: MUSTANG, once an autonomous region, now an enclave of Nepal projecting into Tibet, has long held a fascination for adventurous dreamers. Tibetan culture survives among the villages and in the walled capital, Lo Monthang. The landscape is, apparently, rich with remarkable features: pillars of sandstone, medieval castles, ancient, dusty moraines and stony terraces. For many years it was designated a restricted area, but late in 1991 restrictions were lifted and it is now a highly-prized destination for trekkers.

2: THE THAK KHOLA (Kali Gandaki) is a remarkable river. Rising on the edge of the Tibetan plains, for millions of years it has managed to keep pace with the cataclysmic forces that built, and continue to build, the Himalaya, and has forced its way through the mountains as fast as they have risen. (It has been estimated that the Indian tectonic plate is still moving north at a rate of about 5 centimetres a year, while the mountains are growing annually by about a millimetre.) So, while the mountains are still rising, the Kali Gandaki steadfastly pursues its southerly course, and where it flows between Dhaulagiri and Annapurna it is now an astonishing 6 vertical kilometres ($3^{1}/_{2}$ miles) below their summits. Neither Dhaulagiri nor the Annapurna Himal, then, act as a watershed, for the Kali Gandaki flows undeterred all the way through from north to south. It is interesting to note that before the continental collision took place which gave birth to the Himalaya, Tibet had consisted of well-watered plains. But being deprived of its rainfall by the rising Himalayan mountain wall, it

Tibetan traders set out their wares beside the trail in the upper Thak Khola

gradually turned into the high, cold desert witnessed today.

3: DHAULAGIRI means the "white mountain"; an apt name. This, the seventh highest in the world, is a huge, graceful peak measuring 8167m (26,795ft). Maurice Herzog's French expedition of 1950 initially set out with the aim of finding a route to its summit, but after a lengthy reconnaissance they decided it was too dangerous and turned their attentions to Annapurna instead. (Good descriptions of this reconnaissance are contained in Herzog's highly recommended book, *Annapurna*.) There were six further attempts on Dhaulagiri in the following decade, but it was not until 1960 that a Swiss expedition, which included in its numbers the experienced Austrian mountaineer, Kurt Diemburger, finally won through. The expedition on this occasion began by being airlifted onto the North-east Col at 5877 metres (19,281ft)! On May 13th Diemburger, Diener, Forrer, Schelbert and the Sherpas Nyima Dorji and Nawang Dorji reached the summit. Two other members of the team also reached the top 10 days later. Between 1950 and 1978 no less than 16 expeditions had tried to climb Dhaulagiri; only four of these were successful, but sixteen lives had been lost in the attempts. In 1969, for example, seven members of a strong expedition from the USA tackling a route on the South-east Ridge were killed by an avalanche from the notorious Dhaulagiri icefall.

STAGE 11:

JOMOSOM - TUKUCHE - KALOPANI

Distance:	**20 kilometres (12¹/₂ miles)**
Time:	**5¹/₂-6 hours**
Start altitude:	**2713m (8901ft)**
Low point:	**Kalopani 2530m (8301ft)**
Descent:	**183m (600ft)**
Accommodation:	**Lodges in Marpha, Tukuche, Khobang, Larjung and Kalopani**

On this stage of the trek you pass directly below Dhaulagiri whose summit is more than 5600 metres (18,000ft) above the river. Yet this will be difficult to comprehend, for so close to its base does the route go that the mountain is seriously foreshortened. One needs to be able to stand back several kilometres, to be able to view the full base-to-summit stature of this magnificent peak in order truly to appreciate its size.

On the other, eastern side of the valley the Nilgiri summits gleam like polished diamonds in the sun. These are themselves over 4000 metres (13,000ft) above the valley bed, but again, one has no real concept of scale. The enormity of this tremendous valley and its majestic mountain walls casts both a sense of awe and a shadow of bewilderment on those who have the good fortune to wander through it.

And then, as you enter Kalopani at the end of the day's walk, so Annapurna I holds the sky.

But it's not only the mountains that make today's walk so special. There are the villages too, some of which are the finest in all the Annapurna region. Marpha, for example, is a delightful place - and with some of the best Thakali lodges here it would be no bad thing to choose to stay for a night's lodging. So too might be said of Tukuche, or of Khobang. Architectural interest will be lifted by these neat villages, while views that are experienced along the trail will encourage keen photographers to get through rather a lot of film.

For much of the way it would be possible to walk in the bed of the valley, leaping the occasional rivulet that snakes through. Caution is required when crossing the broad tributary valley of the Ghatte Khola below Larjung, though, for there are no bridges and some of the braided streams may be too wide to leap. It's quite possible that you may have to wade some of these. Below the Ghatte Khola the trail divides and you can choose whether to continue on the west side or cross to the east bank as far as Kalopani.

Before leaving Jomosom it is important to ensure that your trekking permit is checked at the police post which is set beside the main trail at the southern end of town, not far from the airstrip, but on the west (right) bank of the river. In Jomosom, then, you should cross to the right bank of the Thak Khola and continue through town on the broad track which, once outside, rises a little and in about 30 minutes leads across the tributary valley of the Syang Khola (the river is bridged). Across the bridge you enter **SYANG** whose outskirts are fertile with small terraced fields and dotted with trees.

The trail continues along the west bank of the valley with the huge wall extending from Dhaulagiri apparently blocking any exit to the south. This is, of course, an illusion for the river carves an exit at its very base. Along the trail electricity poles mark the route, but appear utterly incongruous in such a setting.

MARPHA (2667m: 8750ft 1¹/₂hrs *accommodation, refreshments*) is a most attractive village whose narrow streets are paved with large flat slabs of stone under which rushing water can be heard - a rare drainage system in these mountains. Some of the lodges alongside the main street have inner courtyards and upper, sheltered restaurants that offer additional interest with their views to the Nilgiri peaks opposite, and out into the street where a constant procession of villagers, trekkers, Tibetan traders and pack animals wander by. Marpha has several shops, including one advertising boot repairs; there's also a post office, library and an important *gompa*. At either end of the village you pass through a decorated Buddhist *kani*.

Outside Marpha the trail continues along the right bank of the valley, first among orchards and past an agricultural development which dates from 1966, then through more wild country. About 45 minutes from the village the trail rounds a bend to be rewarded with yet another wonderful view of Dhaulagiri. Some 15 minutes later you enter (1) **TUKUCHE** (2591m: 8501ft 2¹/₂hrs *accommodation,* *refreshments*). This is a large, two-part village divided by an open flat meadow. Several lodges and shops are located in the second half beyond the meadow.

South of Tukuche cross the mouth of a small valley and over several rivulets along the trail. Then you have a choice of either following the main trail against the lower slopes of the right-hand mountains, or walking along the river bed itself. If you choose the latter, follow the trodden path which leads to easy crossings of numerous streams that feed into the Thak Khola. The main trail is a switchback offering good views at every turn.

About 45 minutes from Tukuche you come to a line of willows with close views up to Dhaulagiri, now towering almost overhead, and across the valley to the west face of the Nilgiri peaks, the "blue mountains". Then you enter **KHOBANG** (2560m: 8399ft 3hrs 15mins *accommodation, refreshments*) a most unusual village whose houses are located from a central tunnel which passes through the settlement. Trekkers with large backpacks may need to duck low beneath some sections of this tunnel roof. As you wander through, half-opened doorways show into the inner courtyards of village houses. The village was apparently designed with this tunnel effect in order to protect the houses from the strong winds that sweep through the valley.

Between Khobang and **LARJUNG** (2550m: 8366ft 3¹/₂hrs *accommodation, refreshments*) the trail forks by a mani wall. Take the left branch, cross a wooden bridge and you will come to a few more lodges.

The trail now becomes a switchback among pinewoods and with huge snow and ice-plastered peaks rising ahead and across the valley. Rounding a bluff the trail descends to a vast amphitheatre of mountains created by the mass of Dhaulagiri, and coming from it the broad tributary valley of the (2) Ghatte Khola which has to be crossed. As there are no proper bridges it is worth studying the vague trail that leads across. It is not always easy to find, although you may see other trekkers and porters working a route over. If you don't mind wading the streams, okay. But if you aim to stay dry, you'll need to scout to and fro to find the most convenient places to cross the many meandering streams that snake through the stony bed. You'll possibly find some have stepping stones or temporary log "bridges" laid across them. A walking stick will aid balance where these are wet.

Locate the main valley trail on the south side of the Ghatte Khola. It climbs again among pines, and a few moments later brings you to a large suspension bridge that crosses the Kali Gandaki (now assuming its better-known name) at a narrowing of the valley where it begins to make a severe leftward curve. Again you have a choice of routes. That which continues along the west bank takes the broad curve of the river beneath the towering mass of Dhaulagiri and joins the other trail where it crosses back to the west bank on the outskirts of Kalopani.

The alternative trail, and the one which most trekkers take, crosses the suspension bridge to the east bank, climbs round the right-hand edge of a pine-covered bluff and descends to the settlement of **KOKETANI** *(refreshments)*. Continuing southward the trail climbs a slope on broad stone steps then divides. Take the right-hand option and about 30 minutes later you pass below a line of houses at **DHAMPU**. Continue ahead for 10 minutes. The valley narrows and you reach another suspension bridge, which you cross to the right bank. From here you gain a remarkable view up to Annapurna I. Bear left and soon enter **KALOPANI** (2530m: 8301ft) where there are several lodges.

Points of Interest Along the Way:

1: TUKUCHE is the village which Maurice Herzog chose as the site for the French expedition's valley base in 1950, and from where the reconnaissance parties set out in search of a route up Dhaulagiri. Before they left France, the President of the Himalayan Committee backing the expedition described Tukuche as "the Chamonix of Nepal". There will be few visitors to Tukuche today who, knowing the busy resort of Chamonix at the base of Mont Blanc, would recognise that as a valid description! It is, however, an interesting small town which, in the past, was an important meeting place for Tibetan traders and those from the south who used the large meadowland between its two distinct sections for their trading ventures. Although Tukuche has lost much of its former trading importance due to the Chinese invasion of Tibet, it looks to trekkers to make up its lost income. The Thakalis here manage some comfortable lodges and there's fine mountain scenery on all sides.

Local orchards ensure that fresh fruit is available, and a *rakshi* made from home-grown fruit is a village speciality. Experienced trekkers with time to spare could take a trail up the steep northern hillside to the Dhampus Pass (or Thapa Pass) at 5250m (17,224ft) between Tukuche Peak and Thapa Peak, for some stunning views. West of the pass lies Hidden Valley, and above that French Pass. Tents and food would be needed to tackle this side-trip as there are no facilities on the way.

2: THE GHATTE KHOLA emerges from a vast amphitheatre blocked by the east-facing walls of Dhaulagiri. Dhaulagiri I is the peak high above to the left. The North-east Col, on which the Swiss expedition of 1960 landed their single-engined Pilatus Porter aircraft, is the dip in the centre, and to the right of that the ridge climbs to Tukuche Peak (6920m: 22,703ft). Thakali herdsmen used to take their animals to pasture in the high meadows upstream, and their steeply climbing trails may be used to approach the notorious Dhaulagiri icefall - but do not stray too close as falling seracs constitute a permanent source of danger. It's a long, steep walk, and you'll need to be equipped for an overnight camp if you plan to explore here. The upper meadows, apparently, make a fine site from which to view the alpenglow on Annapurna.

STAGE 12:
KALOPANI - DANA - TATOPANI

Distance:	**20 kilometres (12¹/₂ miles)**
Time:	**6¹/₂ hours**
Start altitude:	**2530m (8301ft)**
Low point:	**Tatopani 1189m (3901ft)**
Descent:	**1341m (4400ft)**
Accommodation:	**Lodges in Lete, Ghasa, Pairothapla, Kopchepani, Dana and Tatopani**

This stage is long and quite strenuous with lots of switchbacks to the trail, but there are several villages along the way where the route could be conveniently broken if required.

Having passed through the great Himalayan Divide views are no longer dominated by Dhaulagiri. Instead, its folding ridges and spurs form the right-hand wall to the valley, while the enchanting block of the Annapurnas once more holds one's attention off to the left. However, sometimes you're walking on the left bank of the Kali Gandaki and the most spectacular mountains are partially hidden from sight until you resume again on the right bank. On this descent the way enters a more tropical region; vegetation is no longer basically alpine, but grows somewhat rampant and colourful; the air becomes much warmer. Village houses change from the flat-roofed, Tibetan-style buildings of the upper valley, to dwellings with sloping roofs that signify a rainfall area. Monkeys may be seen in the forests and there's more evidence of birdlife.

Between Ghasa and Dana the trail is subject to landslides and the following description may no longer strictly apply to that section. It is a volatile region. The route described travels along the left (east) bank, since that is where the path went when the route was being surveyed. But sometimes the right-hand (west bank) trail is the one to take. If so, it will probably be a little shorter than that described, but remember, you'll not have an opportunity to break the journey at either Pairothapla or Kopchepani.

Kalopani and (1) **LETE** (2438m: 7999ft *accommodation, refreshments*) almost merge. At the northern end of Lete there is a police post where permits will be checked. Nearby are a number of Western-style buildings, while the trail through the lower part of the village is paved and has typical Nepalese dwellings alongside. Views across to Annapurna are very fine from here.

Below the village the trail leads through a lovely stand of pine trees, then descends steeply to the **NAMASTE LODGE** (40mins *accommodation, refreshments*) and a suspension bridge that crosses the Lete Khola draining from the right. Over this the way climbs a series of stone steps, crosses a landslide area and, climbing and falling in regular succession, continues to **GHASA** (2013m: 6604ft 2hrs *accommodation, refreshments*). Ghasa is a three-part village and the most southerly of those in the valley inhabited by Thakalis. The middle part is best. It is paved and with a stream running through; some of the buildings stand on stilts, others are of more solid stone construction. Off to the right is a pleasant waterfall.

Out of Ghasa descend to the gorge of the Kali Gandaki and cross

The trail above Jharkot (Circuit. Stage 10: Pilgrim Trail. Stage 8)

A frail looking bridge over the Khali Gandaki, near Dana
(Circuit. Stage 12: Pilgrim Trail, Stage 6)

the river by another suspension bridge. Now on the left bank the trail switchbacks high above the river, sometimes a little exposed. Pass a few tea-houses and about one hour from Ghasa come to **PAIROTHAPLA** (3hrs *accommodation, refreshments)*, a small settlement with a lodge and a trailside shop. Pass more tea-houses and then make a long, steep and rough descent to **KOPCHEPANI** (3hrs 45mins *accommodation, refreshments*).

At the time of writing the continuing trail to Dana has been affected by more landslips and a new (temporary?) trail created. This slants steeply uphill at the entrance to Kopchepani. It is a narrow trail and at the top of the initial rise levels out to pass a few houses before making the descent towards Dana. From the high point a good balcony view is afforded of the valley ahead and below. Across on the other side of the valley you can see the cascades of Rupse Chhaharo with the small village almost below them which shares the same name. The west bank trail can also be seen from this point. (If the original trail from Kopchepani is reopened, instead of climbing above it you will pass through the village and soon after cross the river to Rupse Chhaharo, then follow the west bank trail down-valley to Dana.)

About one hour from Kopchepani wander through a small village and then cross to the right bank of the Kali Gandaki, turn left and come to **DANA** (1446m: 4744ft 5hrs *accommodation, refreshments*). This large village has shops, post office, police check post and, in its middle section which is reached across a wide stream-bed, a few lodges. The architecture here is markedly different from that of other villages visited along the trail; a number of buildings are three storeys high and have ornately carved windows.

The trail continues down the west side of the valley among low terraced fields and exotic vegetation, and in a little under 10 minutes comes to the third and last part of Dana which also has lodge accommodation. Beyond it another side stream is crossed by suspension bridge and, passing through a small settlement, in about 35 minutes comes to the collection of tea-houses of **GUITE** (5hrs 45mins *refreshments*). A large suspension bridge here crosses the Kali Gandaki, but you ignore this and continue along the right bank,

Nilgiri South (6839m), (Circuit: Stage 13. Pilgrim Trail: Stage 3)

rising and falling against the steep mountainside. Looking back there are splendid views to Nilgiri South (6839m: 22,438ft) and to Annapurna I rising high and majestic across the valley.

TATOPANI (1189m: 3901ft) is reached soon after. A busy, popular village with plenty of lodge accommodation and a street lined with an assortment of shops, it makes a good place to rest for a day or two, to soak in the hot springs (no soap please), to refuel with some of the best food of the trail (garden restaurants with extensive menus), and generally to take things easy before setting out on the long climb to Ghorapani. There is a post office next to the village school and a police check post at the southern end of the main street.

Points of Interest Along the Way:

1: LETE offers two interesting options for experienced trekkers. The first is an alternative route south which avoids the busy, well-trekked trail through the Kali Gandaki and over the Poon Hill Danda. This alternative trail cuts off to the south-west, climbs to a long southerly spur of Dhaulagiri and eventually descends to Beni at the confluence of the Kali Gandaki and Myagdi Khola rivers. (The Myagdi Khola,

A typical teahouse below Ghasa

incidentally, flows from the west side of Dhaulagiri and has a tempting trail following it all the way to its headwaters below French Pass - see the chapter headed *Other Trek Ideas*.) A guide will be necessary for trekkers choosing the route from Lete to Beni, and you will need to carry camping equipment and food. The second option from Lete worth considering, time and energy permitting, would be to cross the Kali Gandaki to gain the village of Chhoya on the eastern side. From here it would be possible to climb a steep trail over a col, named by Herzog's expedition as the Pass of April 27, and continue to the North Annapurna Base Camp in the valley of the Miristi Khola. Again, a guide would be needed, as would camping equipment and food for about a week - which is how long the round trip, Lete to Lete, would take. Both route options provide wonderful views.

STAGE 13:
TATOPANI - SIKHA - GHORAPANI

Distance:	14 kilometres (8¹/₂ miles)
Time:	5¹/₂-6 hours
Start altitude:	1189m (3901ft)
High point:	Ghorapani Deurali 2855m (9367ft)
Height gain:	1666m (5466ft)
Accommodation:	Lodges in Ghara, Sikha, Phalante, Chitre and Ghorapani

Leaving the valley of the Kali Gandaki just below Tatopani, the route now makes a long and tiring climb to the crest of the Poon Hill Danda at Ghorapani Deurali. It's a hard day's trek, but as ever it is visually rewarding. There are numerous resting places (chautaara) erected for laden porters, but which are of equal value to weary trekkers, and plenty of tea-houses along the trail too. There are lodges that exploit the views and tempt you to break the journey into a two-day climb - no bad thing, if you have time to do so. Views north are glorious, for as you gain height so the countryside spreads open; you lose the restrictions imposed by the valley below and are presented with an ever-expanding panorama stimulated by the steep, jagged peaks of Nilgiri South and the huge dome of Dhaulagiri with the deepening trench of the Kali Gandaki running between.

Once more the trail climbs among rhododendron forests and cultivated hillsides carved into terraces. The vegetation is exotic and villages rise in scattered groupings among trees and shrubs lively with birdsong. These villages are inhabited by Magars; agriculturalists by tradition, a number of Magars have also travelled the world as Gurkha soldiers.

Ghorapani is a two-part village; Ghorapani Deurali is a collection of lodges on the very crest of the Poon Hill Danda (Deurali means "pass"); while the "other" Ghorapani lies in a forest clearing a little below on the southern side of the ridge. Poon Hill itself rises to the west of Ghorapani Deurali and is one of Nepal's most famous viewpoints. Given clear skies it is a magnificent place from which to view sunset over the mountains and, equally fine, sunrise too.

Tatopani lies in a narrowing of the Kali Gandaki just north of that river's confluence with the Ghar Khola. Leaving Tatopani heading south the trail climbs a stairway of stone steps and then comes to a long suspension bridge over the river. Cross to the left bank, pass through a small village named after the **GHAR KHOLA** (1173m: 3848ft), cross a second bridge and, at a group of buildings *(refreshments)* break away from the main trail and take a path which climbs to the left. (The lower trail follows the Kali Gandaki to Beni for an alternative route back to Pokhara.)

Having now left the Kali Gandaki the route climbs a steep hillside lush with terraced fields and exotic trees. The trail soon forks. Take the right-hand option and ascend a formidable stairway of stone slabs that appears to be almost endless. Fortunately there are a few tea-houses and *chautaaras* that provide welcome resting places along the trail.

About 1¹/₂ hours from Tatopani the trail emerges from forest shade and comes onto the ridge of Durkun Danda at **SANTOSH HILL** *(refreshments)* with a tea-house settled on the very ridge offering lovely views to both north and south.

Cross the ridge and follow the continuing trail to a settlement a few minutes away, and climb once more to reach **GHARA** (1768m: 5801ft 2¹/₂hrs *accommodation, refreshments*). This busy village has one or two lodges and shops, but is more noteworthy for the magnificent view it commands of Dhaulagiri. The trail maintains its steadfast climb for another 45 minutes to reach **SIKHA** (1920m: 6299ft 3hrs

15mins *accommodation, refreshments*).

Sikha is a substantial village built on ascending levels. The lower part has tea-houses; the upper section lines a ridge 15 minutes above and has a few lodges and simple shops - and once more commands a superb panorama, not just to the big mountains, but down over a glorious landscape of textured, layered hills, terraced and patterned with great artistry.

Above and below Sikha there are one or two notorious landslide areas, caused by a combination of over-worked land, monsoon rains and a steep, unstable hillside. No sooner has one landslip settled than a pathway is carved across it, thus keeping this important and busy route open.

Climbing through terraces above Sikha, in 45 minutes you will come to another tea-house and, eventually, reach **PHALANTE** (2256m: 7402ft 4hrs 45mins *accommodation, refreshments)*, a small village with one or two lodges and a large school. Just 20 minutes or so beyond this the trail brings you to the New Dhaulagiri Lodge on the edge of (1) **CHITRE** (2316m: 7598ft 5hrs 10mins *accommodation, refreshments*). There are several other lodges here and, at a trail junction, a sign indicating a route off to the left which goes to Ghandrung.

From Chitre to the ridge of the Poon Hill Danda involves a steady climb of about an hour through forest of oak and rhododendron. The trail is muddy in places and deeply cut by the strings of pack animals that daily ply this route.

So reach (2) **GHORAPANI DEURALI** (2855m: 9367ft) where there are numerous lodges, shops and a police check post. To locate the "other" Ghorapani cross the ridge and continue on the trail as it descends through more forest for another five minutes or so. That too has a number of lodges.

Points of Interest Along the Way:

1: CHITRE sits at a junction of paths. The main Tatopani-Ghorapani "trade route" passes directly through the village, but there is another trail which heads off to the south-east and is marked with a sign to Ghandrung. Trekkers who wish to travel a less-walked path to either the Annapurna Sanctuary or out to Pokhara, should consider taking this. It leads to a pass, simply named Deurali, in the eastern extension of the Poon Hill Danda where there are one or two lodges, then down to Ghandrung and on to Pokhara. An additional alternative avoids Ghandrung and veers off to Chhomrong in order to visit the Sanctuary. Both options are well-stocked with lodges and tea-houses.

2: GHORAPANI DEURALI must be one of the most-visited places in the Annapurna region. A few years ago the pass was simply known as a watering place for the caravans of pack-horses that regularly crossed the ridge at this point. (Ghorapani means "horse water"). Now it is a crowded ridge-top collection of lodges becoming more numerous each year to cope with the ever-growing demand for accommodation. Above to the west rises Poon Hill (3198m: 10,492ft), a classic viewpoint reached in little over half an hour from the pass. Stunning views from the crown of the hill are enjoyed by hundreds of trekkers every season. These views look to Dhaulagiri, Annapurna, Hiunchuli and Machhapuchhare, soft in the evening alpenglow, crisp in the glory of daybreak. The standard route out to Pokhara descends the southern side of the ridge, but there are two alternative routes worth considering. The first is not often trekked, and leads south-westward along the Poon Hill Danda for two days until you cross the Modi Khola near Kusma, and a further two days of trekking roughly eastwards leads to Pokhara. The second alternative route is a variation of the option given above from Chitre. Leaving Ghorapani Deurali head east along the continuing ridge (much up and down) to Deurali, then down either to Ghandrung and Pokhara, or across to Tadapani and Chhomrong in order to visit the Sanctuary. This last route is given in more detail below. (See route descriptions for the Annapurna Sanctuary.)

STAGE 14:
GHORAPANI - ULLERI - BIRETHANTI

Distance:	12 kilometres (7½ miles)
Time:	5-6 hours
Start altitude:	2855m (9367ft)
Low point:	Birethanti 1097m (3599ft)
Descent:	1758m (5768ft)
Accommodation:	Ghorapani, Nyathanti, Banthanti, Ulleri, Tirkhedhunga, Hille and Birethanti

The southern slopes of the Poon Hill Danda lead to a world very different from that of the Kali Gandaki. Gone are near views of Dhaulagiri and Nilgiri, for the landscape is now dominated by green hills with higher, snow-covered peaks beyond. Gone is the stark regimentation of bare rock and hanging glacier, and the frosty river gorge is no more than a memory as you descend into a sub-tropical climate where agriculture becomes the dominant theme.

The descent to Birethanti is a tiring one. There are thousands of stone steps creating a stairway below Ulleri, but the forests are rich in birdlife and there are waterfalls and streams and splendid views to concentrate on. Handsome villages and many tea-houses break the walk, and you will meet growing numbers of trekkers and porters fresh out of Pokhara sweating as they ascend the steep trail.

It would be prudent for solo trekkers to walk in the company of others all the way out to Pokhara from Ghorapani. Although incidents of mugging are happily still rare in Nepal, the well-trekked trails two or three days out of Pokhara have gained a reputation for this type of activity, and whilst there is no need for alarm, you should take the precaution of not walking alone. It should be stressed, though, that the likelihood of being attacked here is considerably less than might be expected in many towns or cities of the "civilised" West.

From Ghorapani Deurali descend the broad clear trail south of the ridge and in five minutes come to the lower collection of lodges at **GHORAPANI** *(accommodation, refreshments)*, the original village that has been somewhat overtaken by the crowded development at the pass. Through rhododendron and oak forests the way leads down to **NYATHANTI** (2606m: 8550ft 35mins *accommodation, refreshments*), a number of lodges in a clearing, and about an hour later reaches the settlement of **BANTHANTI** (2307m: 7569ft 1¹/₂hrs *accommodation, refreshments*). Banthanti means literally "the place in the forest" and there is another with the same name farther to the east on the trail which leads from Ghorapani to Tadapani.

Between Banthanti and Ulleri the way takes you out of forest and into a region of cultivation. **ULLERI** (2073m: 6801ft 2¹/₂hrs *accommodation, refreshments*) is an attractive village of slate-roofed houses on the right flank of the deep valley of the Bhurungdi Khola, with stupendous views down into it where terraced hillsides are reminiscent of those that so dominated the first day or so of the trek out of Besisahar. Other views look towards Annapurna South and Hiunchuli. The landscape is now becoming more settled, an open, smiling countryside with many tea-houses and lodges.

Below Ulleri the descent is a seemingly endless stairway of almost 4000 steps leading to the bed of the valley. But if you find this a tiring way to descend, have pity on those who are ascending! It will take a little over an hour to reach the river which you cross on a small suspension bridge and enter **TIRKHEDUNGA** (1577m: 5174ft 3hrs 45mins *accommodation, refreshments*). Some of the lodges here advertise that they are run by ex-Gurkha soldiers. **HILLE** (1524m: 5000ft *accommodation, refreshments*) is reached a few minutes later.

The trail descends more gently through well-farmed country, passes through another settlement just over an hour from Hille, and 30 minutes later comes to **BIRETHANTI** (1097m: 3599ft).

This busy, attractive village nestles at the confluence of the Bhurungdi Khola and the larger valley of the Modi Khola which drains out of the Annapurna Sanctuary. Birethanti is an obvious place to spend the night. It has plenty of lodges and shops, a police check post and even a bank with a shotgun-toting guard. Some of the lodges have pleasant dining areas overlooking the river. Vegetation is now sub-tropical, and if you find that the dust of the last few days needs rinsing off, there is a tempting pool in the Bhurungdi river upstream of the village, below a waterfall. A tea-house is situated nearby.

From Birethanti an alternative trail heads up the Modi Khola, along the riverside at first, and then climbs a stone stairway to the important village of Ghandrung (Ghandruk) where the ACAP headquarters is housed. From there a choice of routes offer options of either continuing towards the Annapurna Sanctuary, or crossing the Modi Khola and heading for Pokhara by way of Landrung.

STAGE 15:
BIRETHANTI - LUMLE - SUIKHET - POKHARA

Distance:	**24 kilometres (15 miles)**
Time:	**2 hours (Lumle) 4¹⁄₂ hours (Suikhet) 5 hours (Pokhara - with transport from Suikhet)**

Start altitude:	**1097m (3599ft)**
Low point:	**Pokhara 819m (2687ft)**
Height gain:	**518m (1699ft)**
Descent:	**278m (912ft)**
Accommodation:	**Lodges in Chandrakot, Lumle, Khare, Naudanda and Pokhara**
Transport options:	**Truck (Lumle to Suikhet - or possibly bus to Pokhara) Bus or taxi (Suikhet to Pokhara)**

Nepal is sprouting roads. One of these has pushed out of Pokhara and is heading for Baglung in the lower valley of the Kali Gandaki south of Beni. At Lumle our route comes across this road, which has destroyed some of the charm of the walk out to Pokhara. A sign here announces "Beginning of Trekking" so Lumle might justifiably be considered the end of the Annapurna Circuit. Walking along the road will not be very pleasant when traffic is using it. At the time of writing it was not open to general traffic, and the only alternative to walking was to hope for a lift on one of the contractor's trucks as far as Suikhet - an option guaranteed to cover you with a film of white dust from the unsurfaced road. At Suikhet it is possible either to catch a bus into Pokhara, or to hire a taxi for the final run into town, but it is quite likely that transport will soon be available all the way from Lumle. The valley route beyond Suikhet passes the Tibetan settlement of Hyangja and enters Pokhara from the north.

For those who prefer to walk all the way, a brief description of the route is given.

Leave Birethanti by way of the suspension bridge over the Modi Khola and continue on a pleasant riverside walk for about 20 minutes before turning uphill for an unrelieved ascent to **CHANDRAKOT** (1600m: 5249ft 1¹/₂hrs *accommodation, refreshments*). This pleasant hilltop village enjoys spectacular views of Annapurna South, Hiunchuli and Machhapuchhare at the head of the Modi Khola's valley. In the early morning these views are especially clear and will create an unforgettable impression. But gazing south you will see far below the new road to Baglung, and for the first time since leaving Besisahar, motor vehicles.

Heading east the trail leads through a cultivated landscape with delightful views of the Annapurna massif off to your left, and in half an hour comes to **LUMLE** (1615m: 5299ft 2hrs *accommodation, refreshments*). The main street through the village is paved with stone slabs and lined with lodges, and with the coming of the road marks an obvious end to the trek. A British-run agricultural project based here trains ex-Gurkha soldiers in farming practices.

For the continuing route out to Pokhara, whether or not you hope for a lift, follow the road as it heads uphill roughly south-east, passes through the small hilltop village of **KHARE** *(accommodation, refreshments)* and then descends with distant views of Pokhara's lake. As the road bears right, take a well-trodden short-cut left to **NAUDANDA** (1425m: 4675ft *accommodation, refreshments*) a long straggling village noted for its views. With the coming of the road the village has lost much of its former attraction. The road now cuts down left with a series of zig-zags, while numerous footpath short-cuts lead to **SUIKHET** (1113m: 3652ft 4^1/$_2$hrs *refreshments*).

At Suikhet buses and taxis wait for trekkers hoping for a ride to Pokhara. However, those who prefer to walk all the way should follow the ridge heading south-east from Naudanda towards Sarangkot. A little over half an hour from Naudanda bear right on a trail that drops to the western end of Pokhara's lake, Phewa Tal - about 2^1/$_2$ hours from Naudanda, 6^1/$_2$ hours from Birethanti. It is then possible to finish the journey by boat to Pokhara.

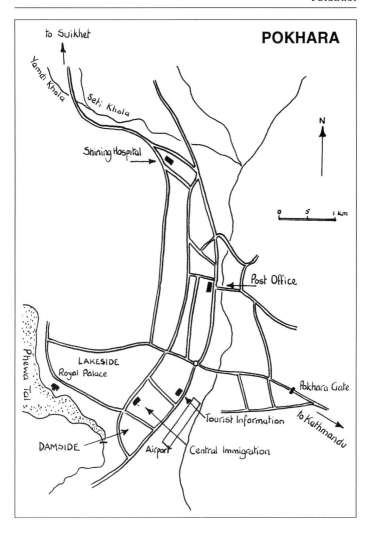

THE ANNAPURNA SANCTUARY

Big mountains heaved to heaven which the blinding sunsets blazon,
Black canyons where the rapids rip and roar. (Robert Service)

The Annapurna Sanctuary is one of the most scenically dramatic mountain amphitheatres imaginable. Picture an almost complete ring of high peaks, eight of which top 7000 metres (23,000ft), draped with snowfields and glaciers, with stern buttresses and ice flutings that thrust heavenwards from a rough, undulating basin. Imagine, there is only one way into this basin, and that entails a trek through a gorge clothed with dense bamboo jungle and rain forest that, combined with the great shafting walls of the gorge, effectively captures the mists and denies access to the sun for much of the day. Deep within this gorge thunders the Modi Khola, a river composed of the melt of all glaciers and snowfields trapped within the Sanctuary itself.

Picture the moonrise over these mountains. Imagine rising from a high camp among them, or emerging from a lodge or tent at over 4000 metres (13,000ft) to be greeted by the brilliance of their ice-coated flanks lit by the morning sun; of delicate cornices picked out against the deep blue of a Himalayan sky. Imagine hour after hour of unadorned majesty that is suddenly snatched from your field of vision by the mid-day clouds that boil up from the hidden gorge as if from a witch's cauldron. There is beauty and drama in that too.

All this, and much much more, awaits the trekker who heads through the "gates" of the Sanctuary between Hiunchuli and Machhapuchhare and wanders the trail that rises another 400 metres (1300ft) or so to reach the panoramic area known as Annapurna Base Camp.

For generations Gurung shepherds had taken their flocks to summer pasture in the Sanctuary, but it was not until 1956 that the first Westerner penetrated the gorge of the Modi Khola and gazed at those scenes of great beauty. J.O.M."Jimmy" Roberts, then a Gurkha officer and later Military Attaché at the British Embassy in Kathmandu, was on reconnaissance for the only expedition to be sanctioned for an attempt to climb Machhapuchhare. (The attempt was made the following year during which Wilfred Noyce and David Cox reached a point about 50 metres (160ft) below the summit.) It was Roberts who named this great cauldron of peaks the Annapurna Sanctuary; an appropriate name since it was considered sacred by the Gurungs who lived nearby. As if to reinforce the sanctity of the area he had to deposit 50 eggs at a small shrine in the gorge in order to pacify the gods who dwelt there. (At the time eggs, chicken and pork were forbidden beyond the shrine - as were women - for fear of upsetting the deities of the Sanctuary.)

After the Machhapuchhare expedition a slow trickle of mountaineers followed the trail through the Modi Khola's gorge. One early group was a Japanese team which climbed Glacier Dome (Tarke Kang 7193m: 23,599ft) in 1964, while a year later a German expedition led by Gunther Hauser made the first ascent of the triangular Gangapurna (7454m: 24,455ft). But without question the most spectacularly successful expedition was Chris Bonington's team which in 1970 made the first ascent of the enormous South Face of Annapurna I from a base camp at around 4000 metres (13,000ft) near the Annapurna glacier - now the site of a couple of trekkers' lodges. The Sanctuary became a focus of attention for trekking parties, and since 1978 has also gained popularity with mountaineers inspired by a number of "trekking peaks" accessible from it.

The Sanctuary makes an undeniably attractive goal. Outstanding high mountain views are on offer during a large part of the approach march, and the contrasts of lowland rice paddies, gloomy jungles of bamboo and dazzling snowpeaks add much to the broad range of experience. The glorious bastions that outline the Sanctuary are seen in full majesty from Pokhara. North of the lake of Phewa Tal they glow of a morning, a perfect snow-bound horizon whose dominant feature is the pinnacle of Machhapuchhare. And along the trail to it this graceful virgin summit appears and reappears with teasing familiarity, soaring beyond the rice paddies, hovering over thatched villages, signalling above the deep, dark gorge.

This trek is a much shorter option than that of the Annapurna Circuit, taking about 10 days in all for the basic round-trip from Pokhara, although there are various options available in order to lengthen it where desired. Suggestions are made below. One of these options, popular with trekkers embarked upon the Circuit, is to visit the Sanctuary on the way out to Pokhara by making a diversion from Ghorapani. This route is also outlined in the following pages. But although the basic trek is a comparatively short one there are some steep ascents and whilst not difficult, the trail is more demanding than a first glance at the map might suggest.

On this trek, as on the Circuit, there are numerous lodges and tea-houses along the way, so in the spring and autumn trekking seasons it would be quite feasible to travel light and rely on food and accommodation at the end of every stage. However, one should remember that for the two days of approach through the gorge of the Modi Khola lodges are liable to be very busy - space being at a premium since the route from Chhomrong to the Sanctuary is used by traffic in both directions.

Another point to consider is the potential danger of avalanche near the overhanging Hinko Cave. This danger is particularly acute in winter and early spring following heavy snowfall when avalanches pour down from the unseen Hiunchuli to cover the trail. If there is any conceivable possibility of avalanche, do not proceed along the gorge - either up or down - until it has passed. On occasion parties of trekkers have found themselves trapped for a few days within the Sanctuary itself, unable to escape until all danger had gone. Bear this in mind when planning your trek and allow enough leeway to accommodate such a time-absorbing delay.

The Sanctuary is a conservation area and parties intending to camp within it are forbidden to use wood for cooking purposes. The same rule applies to all lodges beyond Chhomrong. Chhomrong is the last village before you enter the Modi Khola gorge. Trekkers who aim to be self-sufficient can hire pressure stoves and buy kerosene here for use during the next few days. Enquire at the ACAP check post.

THE ANNAPURNA SANCTUARY

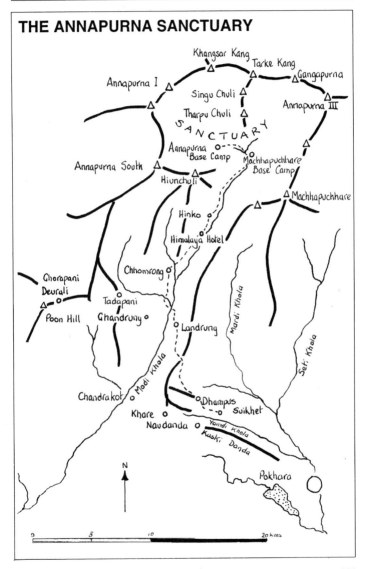

ROUTE PROFILE:
THE ANNAPURNA SANCTUARY

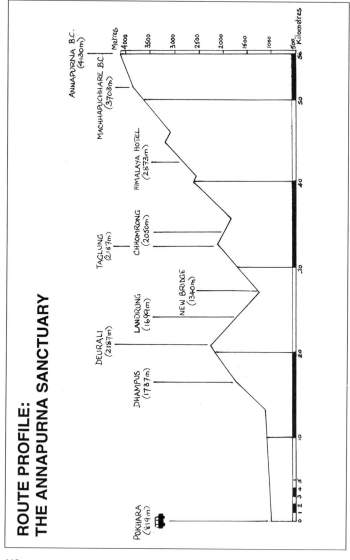

STAGE 1:
POKHARA - DHAMPUS - LANDRUNG

Distance:	**25 kilometres (15½ miles)**
Time:	**5-6 hours (with transport to Suikhet)**
Start altitude:	**819m (2687ft)**
High point:	**Deurali 2187m (7175ft)**
Height gain:	**1368m (4488ft)**
Descent:	**488m (1601ft)**
Accommodation:	**Lodges in Dhampus, Pothana, Tolka and Landrung**
Transport options:	**Bus or taxi (Pokhara to Suikhet)**

The linear distance and amount of height-gain quoted above for this stage suggests a very hard first day, but it is possible to arrange motor transport from Pokhara to Suikhet, in which case the horizontal distance will be halved and in addition you will have saved a little over 300 metres (984ft) of uphill effort. If, however, you decide to walk all the way, add another day to your schedule.

Of the two main outward routes from Pokhara, this is the shortest and most obvious, now that the Chinese road has been built through the valley of the Yamdi Khola north-west of town. Buses and taxis ply the route through the villages of Hyangja and Suikhet and it is worth beginning the trek with a ride to a point just beyond Suikhet, where the real trail now begins.

Even with vehicular support at the start, this will be a tiring first day. There's a lot of height to gain in order to cross the wooded ridge above Pothana, and some sections of the trail are quite steep. Perhaps the worst part is the initial ascent to Dhampus through rice terraces and up a long flight of stone steps that will sorely test your preparations for this trek.

Dhampus has an unwelcome reputation for theft from trekkers. If you are camping, or using a lodge in or near the village, be extra vigilant and never leave your belongings unguarded. If you plan to walk all the way to Landrung on this stage, make sure you have reliable company - especially on the trail through forest above Dhampus and over the ridge. As was pointed out in the trail descriptions for the final stages of the Annapurna Circuit, the incidence of mugging in Nepal, whilst nowhere as bad as in the "civilised" West, has been concentrated on the busy trekking routes within a day or two of the road north of Pokhara. Without becoming neurotic, it would be prudent to keep valuables out of sight and just remain extra vigilant during the first few days.

Take a taxi or bus for the drive from Pokhara to the start of the trail (1128m: 3701ft) a short distance beyond Suikhet. The trail begins just beyond a bridge over a tributary stream, and climbs steeply through sal forest. It can be clearly seen rising ahead on the right-hand (north) side of the road. Above the trees it leads around rice terraces - and sometimes across them when the harvest has been taken. There are various alternative paths, so if in doubt as to the correct one, ask a local for the way to Dhampus.

After about an hour and a half from the road enter the strung-out village of **DHAMPUS** (1737m: 5699ft 2hrs *accommodation, refreshments*) which is settled on a ridge. Rising out of the terraces below the village views had begun to expand ahead, and from Dhampus these views show the high peaks for which you are aiming. There are lodges at both ends of the village, and between the two main sections the trail leads through open country.

Wandering through the upper part of Dhampus the way continues to climb heading west, then becomes a partially-paved route through more forest. There is a major trail junction where you continue ahead, ignoring the left branch which leads to Khare on the popular route to and from Ghorapani. Shortly after this you come to the rather untidy village of **POTHANA** (2034m: 6673ft 3hrs *accommodation, refreshments*). Continuing, wander up to the wooded ridge above the village, follow along it for a short distance and then come to a clearing with some tea-houses. This is **DEURALI** (2187m: 7175ft *refreshments*).

Now the path descends the north slope, still among forest, passes one or two tea-houses and comes to **BERI KHARKA** (4$^{1}/_{2}$hrs *refreshments*). The trail crosses a tumbling stream by a suspension bridge, and before long you emerge from the cover of trees to a broad hillside that has been cultivated in numerous terraces with the valley of the Modi Khola far below.

TOLKA (1821m: 5974ft 4hrs 45mins *accommodation, refreshments*) is a small village along the trail; ahead the larger settlement of Landrung soon comes into view and the views expand again. On the far side of the valley you can see Ghandrung.

LANDRUNG (1699m: 5574ft), also known as Landruk, is an

attractive Gurung village with a paved street and a number of circular thatched houses. There are several lodges and the views to Annapurna South and Hiunchuli are magnificent. The village is set on the steeply sloping hillside and with a considerable height difference between the upper buildings and those at the lower end.

STAGE 2:
LANDRUNG - NEW BRIDGE - CHHOMRONG

Distance:	10 kilometres (6 miles)
Time:	5-5½ hours
Start altitude:	1669m (5476ft)
High point:	Taglung 2187m (7175ft)
Low point:	New Bridge 1340m (4396ft)
Height gain:	847m (2779ft)
Descent:	329m (1079ft)
Accommodation:	Lodges in New Bridge, Jinu, Taglung and Chhomrong

This is a grand day's walk which takes you into the valley of the Modi Khola with enticing views of Annapurna South, Hiunchuli, Gangapurna and Machhapuchhare. It also shows for the first time the extent of the gorge through which you will be trekking during the next two days.

It's an energetic stage with some steep uphill climbs to tackle, but the short riverside trail to New Bridge makes a delightful prelude among rhododendrons before facing the long climb to Taglung.

A variation of this route is possible for those who may be interested in visiting the village of Ghandrung where the ACAP headquarters are situated. It entails dropping from Landrung to the river, then climbing the opposite slope to Ghandrung - a large and important Gurung village on several levels, each of which is higher than Landrung. From there a major trail switchbacks along the western flank of the valley and rejoins our route at Taglung, just before Chhomrong. The Ghandrung-Chhomrong route is briefly outlined below.

Landrung (Landruk) is perched high above the valley, so you begin the day by descending through the village to the trail junction below it near the Himalaya Hotel. The left-hand path immediately descends to the Modi Khola and is the one to take if you plan to visit Ghandrung. The direct route to Chhomrong via New Bridge, however, heads to the right and slopes down through terraces, eventually reaching the heavily vegetated valley bed, which is broken here and there with large boulders. This is the path to take. Once in the valley continue upstream on an easy trail with the Modi Khola to your left, and before long you will pass a few houses and come to a suspension bridge over the river. Above it, on the opposite bank, is the cluster of buildings of **NEW BRIDGE** (1340m: 4396ft 1 hour *accommodation, refreshments*). It was the construction of this suspension bridge, after which the former settlement of Himalkyo is now named, that has made this more direct route to the Sanctuary possible.

Now on the true right bank of the river (west side) you begin to climb to the few houses of **SAMRUNG** (1430m: 4692ft *refreshments*). Just beyond these the way crosses a side stream, makes a rising traverse of steep hillside, then climbs more determinedly to **JINU** (1760m: 5774ft *accommodation, refreshments*) which has access to hot springs, about 15 minutes' walk away.

From here the climb seems relentless, but views to Gangapurna in the Sanctuary provide a good enough excuse for frequent rests. The trail works a way very steeply up a long spur of hillside and at last emerges onto a broad path (the route from Ghandrung and Ghorapani) at the huddle of tea-houses and lodges of **TAGLUNG** (2187m: 7175ft 4hrs 45mins *accommodation, refreshments*). This is also known as Daalu. Bear right and follow the path as it climbs a little, rounds a curve of hillside and there below lies Chhomrong, or Chomro.

CHHOMRONG (2050m: 6726ft) is a busy Gurung village built in two sections on a steep hillside with more than 100 metres (330ft) difference in altitude between the new (upper) and old (lower) villages. A long paved stairway consisting of hundreds of steps links the two, and there are lodges in both parts. Some of these lodges are among the largest and best-kept of the whole Annapurna region, with solar-heated showers and dining rooms with picture windows that gaze out at the fish-tail peak of Machhapuchhare beckoning above the Modi gorge, and at the dominating block of Annapurna South peering down on the valley. There are several shops in the lower village that could be useful for stocking up with food for the days ahead, and the final trekking permit check post on the route to the Sanctuary is located halfway down the paved stairway to it. This is also the ACAP office and kerosene depot where fuel can be bought and pressure stoves rented by those trekkers who plan to camp on the way to, and in, the Sanctuary where open fires are banned.

Whilst in Chhomrong it is worth enquiring of trekkers who have just come from the Sanctuary about conditions on the trail in - with special attention to any avalanche danger that might exist in the gorge near Hinko Cave. If there has been recent heavy snowfall, either abandon your plan to go to the Sanctuary, or wait in Chhomrong until all danger of avalanche has passed before proceeding. Check too about the availability of lodge accommodation. At certain times of the year there will be few, if any, lodges open in either the Modi gorge or in the Sanctuary itself. Those at Machhapuchhare and Annapurna Base Camps are usually closed during winter and off-season trekkers will need to be completely self-sufficient. At other times one or two mentioned below may also be closed, and at peak times there may even be a shortage of supplies getting through, thus affecting the provision of meals. This problem is heightened when the trail has been cut off for some days by avalanche.

Note too that the names of some of the lodges in the gorge, and indeed even their siting, may change from time to time.

STAGE 3:
CHHOMRONG - HIMALAYA HOTEL

Distance:	8 kilometres (5 miles)
Time:	6 hours
Start altitude:	2050m (6726ft)
High point:	Himalaya Hotel 2873m (9426ft)
Low point:	Chhomrong Khola 1890m (6201ft)
Height gain:	983m (3225ft)
Descent:	160m (525ft)
Accommodation:	Lodges in Sinuwa Danda, Kulde, Bamboo Lodge, Tip Top, Doban, Annapurna Approach and Himalaya Hotel

Machhapuchhare above the Modi Khola

Despite the modest linear distance quoted above for this stage, it is a very strenuous day's walking with the trail making a constant switchback through the gorge of the Modi Khola. Some of these switchbacks are very severe - both up and down - and in places the path can be extremely slippery. Trekkers (especially those carrying heavy rucksacks) should take care with their footing. This is just the terrain to cause havoc with weak ankles and knees. On one journey through I met a lady trekker being carried on the back of a porter as her knees had been wrecked by the steep descents.

At first the route gives the possibility of views, but then it heads among rain forests of rhododendron and, later, dense thickets of bamboo. Mists often hang in the valley; the bamboo drips moisture and rivulets and small streams drain across and along the trail, making it muddy in places.

When views are clear they are magnificent and dominated by Annapurna III and Machhapuchhare, which from the gorge has the appearance of the regal fish's tail that gives it its name. But mostly these views are blinkered by the bamboo jungle that crowds the narrow trail.

Since this section of the route is used in both directions by every visitor to the Sanctuary - trekkers, mountaineering expeditions and their porters - it follows that at times bottle-necks occur. Lodges also become heavily used, and all who rely on them for accommodation are advised not to push on too late in the day before booking a bed for the night. As a final word, please do not add to the litter of previous visitors, but do your part in reducing the amount of rubbish deposited in the area by a few of our mindless predecessors.

Beyond Chhomrong the valley forks. The left-hand, western branch has the Chhomrong Khola draining the glaciers of Hiunchuli, while the eastern gorge is that of the Modi Khola through which access is gained to the Sanctuary.

Descend the interminable staircase of steps through Chhomrong to reach a suspension bridge below and to the left of the village (1890m: 6201ft). This crosses the Chhomrong Khola and beyond it the trail begins a long twisting climb up and round the hillside spur which divides the two valleys. Now with the Modi Khola far below the route continues on the western flanks of the valley and passes several tea-houses. Wandering through rain forests of oak and rhododendron, with thickets of bamboo squeezing the trail, you will reach the group of lodges at **SINUWA DANDA** (2360m: 7743ft 1hr 45mins *accommodation, refreshments*).

With persistent switchbacks the trail leads on without respite. **KULDE** (2499m: 8199ft 3hrs *accommodation, refreshments*) has an alternative high trail leading to another lodge on the site of a former British sheep-breeding station, but the main trail suddenly descends steeply with stone steps and enters dense bamboo jungle. In a clearing, about 30 minutes or so below Kulde, you come to the appropriately-named lodges at **BAMBOO** (2339m: 7674ft 3$^{1}/_{2}$hrs *accommodation, refreshments*).

The climb from Bamboo to Himalaya Hotel is less severe than was the earlier part of the walk and makes a steady ascent, albeit with a few short, steep sections. On the way there are several side streams to cross. These are usually aided by large stepping stones or with bamboo poles lashed together to form a bridge. The route continues to be slippery when wet.

TIP TOP LODGE (4hrs *accommodation, refreshments*) stands alone high above the river and looks upvalley to Machhapuchhare. Half an hour beyond it you will come to the lodge of **DOBAN** (2606m: 8550ft 4$^{1}/_{2}$hrs *accommodation, refreshments*), and climbing on, but with welcome level sections, soon reach the **ANNAPURNA APPROACH LODGE** (2646m: 8681ft *accommodation, refreshments*).

More switchbacks and narrow sections of trail lead deeper into the gorge, and about an hour and a half beyond Doban you cross a tributary stream and there in a clearing are the two lodges and camping area of **HIMALAYA HOTEL** (2873m: 9426ft).

STAGE 4:

HIMALAYA HOTEL - MACHHAPUCHHARE BASE CAMP

Distance:	9 kilometres (5^{1}/2 miles)
Time:	3-3^{1}/2 hours
Start altitude:	2873m (9426ft)
High point:	**Machhapuchhare Base Camp 3703m (12,149ft)**
Height gain:	830m (2723ft)
Accommodation:	**Lodges at Hinko Cave, Deurali, Bagar and Machhapuchhare Base Camp**

If it is your intention to combine this stage with the next (the route to Annapurna Base Camp), it is advisable to set out early from Himalaya Hotel - dawn at the latest - in order to reach your destination before clouds come in to swamp all views: a regular phenomenon.

It is on this stage that the trail crosses areas of avalanche danger - the only major trekking route in Nepal to do so. Warnings have already been given with regard to the caution required following heavy snowfall.

On the approach to the Sanctuary, which is entered just below Machhapuchhare Base Camp, you will break free of the visual restrictions of bamboo thickets and make a way through a much more open region. In places the valley is almost alpine, but the scale is greater than anything the Alps can offer. As you rise towards the huge rocky portals that guard the Sanctuary, so Gangapurna's triangular face shines tantalizingly between the steep constricting walls of the gorge to lure you on.

It has to be said that views from Machhapuchhare Base Camp can be rather disappointing. You're too close to the base of Machhapuchhare itself to gain any true perspective, and the vegetated moraine that comes down from Annapurna's glacier effectively bars views to other peaks. Far better is it to climb another 400 metres (1300ft) or so in height to Annapurna Base

Camp for a spectacular panorama. However, it might be deemed more suitable to sleep at this lower site and make a higher foray from it.

Leaving Himalaya Hotel the trail winds up among bamboo thickets and forest, narrow in places and still slippery after rain or snow, then steepens to gain **HINKO CAVE** (3139m: 10,298ft 1 hour *accommodation, refreshments*). Hinko is a uniquely-situated lodge that can sleep about a dozen, and is built tight against a huge overhanging boulder formerly used as a bivouac site by the shepherds and hunters who forced this trail.

Beyond Hinko descend to cross a ravine and climb out on the other side. This is a classic avalanche trap. On occasion the gorge is virtually blocked here, and it is often necessary to climb over the debris brought down from the slopes of Hiunchuli, unseen above to the left. The way continues across several streams and about half an hour from Hinko brings you to the two lodges of **DEURALI** (3231m: 10,600ft 1¹/₂hrs *accommodation, refreshments*).

The valley broadens and there's a change in vegetation as the trail meanders across a fairly level section where Gangapurna shows itself ahead, framed by the steep walls that form the gateway to the Sanctuary. More avalanche chutes are crossed and the path once more climbs against the left-hand mountainside before dropping to **BAGAR** (3300m: 10,827ft 2hrs *accommodation, refreshments*) where there are two small lodges.

Apparently there is an alternative trail on the eastern side of the Modi Khola above Bagar which is used when the normal route is blocked by avalanche. The standard path, however, continues along the western flanks and eventually enters the Sanctuary. A stream pours down from the left and is crossed by a bridge. Immediately in front rises a steep, vegetated bluff on top of which is settled a lodge. This is the first of the buildings of **MACHHAPUCHHARE BASE CAMP**, the others are found a little beyond.

The trail forks. If you wish to stay in the lodge on the bluff take the clear but narrow path which climbs directly ahead. If, however, it is your intention to overnight in one of the other lodges (or continue to Annapurna Base Camp) follow the path which veers left. It skirts the foot of the bluff and forks again. The left branch goes up to Annapurna Base Camp, while a short stroll straight ahead will bring you to the

Fish Tail Lodge, known also as **MACHHAPUCHHARE BASE CAMP** (3703m: 12,149ft).

It was around here that Jimmy Roberts and his small team made their base while attempting to climb Machhapuchhare in 1957; the story of that expedition is told by Wilfred Noyce in *Climbing the Fish's Tail*. Then, in 1970 during his reconnaissance in advance of the successful ascent of the South Face of Annapurna I, Don Whillans made a temporary camp here and he saw first a moving shape, then tracks, that his Sherpas swore belonged to a Yeti. He describes this experience in Chris Bonington's book, *Annapurna South Face*.

Machhapuchhare (6993m: 22,943ft) rises abruptly to your right: a great shaft of rock, snow and ice seriously foreshortened and failing to provide the beautiful fish tail profile for which it is known. Above to the left can be seen Annapurna South (7219m: 23,684ft), but more extensive views are reserved for the belvedere of Annapurna Base Camp.

Annapurna South Face

STAGE 5:

MACHHAPUCHHARE BASE CAMP - ANNAPURNA BASE CAMP

Distance: 4 kilometres (2¹/₂ miles)
Time: 1¹/₂-2 hours
Start altitude: 3703m (12,149ft)
High point: Annapurna Base Camp 4130m (13,550ft)
Height gain: 427m (1401ft)
Accommodation: Lodges at Annapurna Base Camp

The trek to Annapurna Base Camp ascends at a steady gradient, never very steeply, but the altitude is likely to have a tiring effect. Do not hurry, but ascend slowly and enjoy the expanding panorama. The route leads along a trough below the vegetated moraine that edges the unseen South Annapurna glacier. It's a clear, well-defined trail and as you gain height so the lodge buildings can be seen ahead. The final rise to them is the steepest part of the approach.

If you begin this last stage of the route from the Fish Tail Lodge area, simply follow the path which heads west upvalley to join the main trail rising through the centre of the valley. If, however, your approach is from the bluff-top lodge, or a continuation of the route from the Modi Khola's gorge, take the left-hand trail at the fork below and to the left of the lodge just referred to.

This trail rises easily through the undulating trough, or ablation valley, below the glacial moraine, and with the slopes of Hiunchuli rising above to your left. Cross a minor ridge to a flat area with rivulets flowing through and continue heading upvalley with views to Annapurna South now looking grand, and its northern ridge leading towards Annapurna I, which remains frustratingly obscure until almost the last minute. Pause now and then to enjoy the growing views behind, and you will realise just how much altitude is being gained.

ANNAPURNA BASE CAMP (4130m: 13,550ft) is a high level patch rimmed by glacial moraine. It should be noted that this was the base camp site for the South Face of Annapurna, as used by Bonington's 1970 expedition, and not that of Herzog's 1950 base camp which was, of course, located on the northern side of the mountain. There are two lodges here and plenty of camping spaces. It is a cold and often windy spot, but the panorama is nothing short of spectacular. Perhaps the very best views to be had by non-mountaineers are from the crest of the moraine wall just beyond the lodges; a magical place that looks on to soaring buttresses of rock and ice, hanging glaciers, high snowfields, shapely peaks and ridges with cornices diamond clear against the sky. Be warned that often clouds fill the Sanctuary around midday and remain there to deny all views until nightfall.

Because of the altitude of Annapurna Base Camp, and the comparatively short amount of time required to reach it, trekkers slow to acclimatise are likely to suffer headaches and feelings of nausea here. In this event you are strongly advised to descend, at least as far as Machhapuchhare Base Camp. Read the paragraphs on altitude sickness contained in the section entitled *Health Matters* in the Introductory chapters of this book.

The Sanctuary:

The Sanctuary is a dramatically beautiful mountain amphitheatre which makes an almost complete circle, with just the narrow cleft of the Modi Khola's gorge breaking the ring of high peaks. Going clockwise, and beginning in the south, those peaks on view are: Hiunchuli, Annapurna South (Modi Peak), Fang (otherwise Baraha Shikhar), Annapurna I; then Tharpu Chuli (Tent Peak) and Singu Chuli (Fluted Peak) effectively block the continuing rim of the Sanctuary until you gaze on Gangapurna, Annapurna III, the delicate peak of Ghandharba Chuli (Gabelhorn) and Machhapuchhare whose face appears to plunge into a deep, deep well below.

Several mountains within, and on the edge of the amphitheatre, are on the list of designated trekking peaks. (This title is something of a misnomer since high mountaineering experience and equipment will be required in order to tackle them.) These are: Hiunchuli (6441m: 21,132ft), Tharpu Chuli (5663m: 18,580ft), Singu Chuli (6501m: 21,329ft) and Mardi Himal (5587m: 18,330ft), this last-named being an extension of Machhapuchhare and the most southerly of the Annapurna group.

Of these trekking peaks Hiunchuli was first climbed by an American Peace Corps expedition in 1971, Tharpu Chuli by a Japanese

Annapurna III (left) and Ghandharba Chuli from Annapurna Base Ccmp

expedition bound for Annapurna South in 1964, Singu Chuli by Wilfred Noyce and David Cox whilst acclimatising prior to their attempt on Machhapuchhare (1957), and Mardi Himal fell to Jimmy Roberts and two Sherpas in 1961. Those interested to learn more about these peaks should consult Bill O'Connor's book, *The Trekking Peaks of Nepal*.

In time all the larger mountains of the Sanctuary have naturally drawn the attention of full-scale expeditions. The Japanese were among the very first, and were successful here in 1964 when they climbed Tarke Kang (7193m: 23,599ft), perhaps better known as Glacier Dome, and the superb Annapurna South (7219m: 23,684ft).

Annapurna I (8091m: 26,545ft), as has already been mentioned, was the first 8000m mountain to be climbed when Herzog and Lachenal of a French expedition led by Herzog himself reached the summit from the north in 1950. Both Herzog and Lachenal suffered severe frostbite, were forced to bivouac in a crevasse on the way down and only narrowly escaped with their lives. Annapurna's awesome South Face was climbed by Bonington's British expedition in 1970, with Don Whillans and Dougal Haston the summit pair.

Gangapurna (7454m: 24,455ft) was won by a German team led by Gunther Hauser in 1965. The original aim of this expedition was to climb Annapurna I from the Sanctuary, but on appraisal they altered course and decided instead to tackle this fine, hitherto unclimbed peak to the west of Annapurna III.

Annapurna III (7555m: 24,787ft), and its extensive south-projecting ridge which forms one of the embracing arms of the Sanctuary, effectively blocks the eastern part of the massif from view. (Beyond it rise Annapurnas IV and II, and Lamjung Himal.) Annapurna III was climbed in 1961 by an Indian expedition and, as has already been stated, a small British team led by Jimmy Roberts climbed to within 50m of the summit of Machhapuchhare (6993m: 22,943ft) in 1957, since when all further applications to attempt the mountain have been refused by the Nepalese authorities.

ALTERNATIVE ANNAPURNA SANCTUARY TREKS

Whilst the standard trek to the Annapurna Sanctuary from Pokhara is described above, the following outline route suggests a worthy alternative for the walk-in as far as Chhomrong. The second option outlines the route to the Sanctuary for trekkers who have almost completed the Annapurna Circuit. This goes from Ghorapani to Chhomrong. Thereafter the trek through the gorge of the Modi Khola is of necessity the same as that already described. As with the main route, on these alternatives lodges and tea-houses are available throughout and views to the high peaks consistently fine.

1) Pokhara to Chhomrong; via Chandrakot and Ghandrung (3 days)

To walk all the way from Pokhara either take the trail heading up to the intermediate ridge of the Kaski Danda from the lake (Phewa Tal) to reach a point midway between Sarangkot and Naudanda, or wander up the same ridge from its eastern end starting near Pokhara's Shining Hospital. This latter trail reaches **SARANGKOT** and continues along the crest to **NAUDANDA** where there is a police check post and superb views of the Annapurna massif.

An alternative option is to travel by bus or taxi along the valley of the Yamdi Khola. The road now continues beyond Suikhet and Phedi, crosses the Kaski Danda at Naudanda and goes to **LUMLE**. When it is open to traffic it might be worth driving all the way to Lumle, or even beyond, and begin the trek there. In this event you will save a day's walking.

From Naudanda head west to **LUMLE** and **CHANDRAKOT** at the end of the ridge overlooking the valley of the Modi Khola. (Yet another alternative to the route suggested here leaves the ridge at **KHARE**, between Naudanda and Lumle, and heads north on a trail that wanders to **POTHANA** midway between Dhampus and Deurali to join Stage 1 of the main route already described.) From Chandrakot, however, either descend to the river and take a trail upstream from **BIRETHANTI** which leads on the west bank all the way to **GHANDRUNG**, or choose the path which breaks away to the north from Chandrakot, and follows the east flank of the Modi Khola's valley before crossing it by suspension bridge after two hours, and then climbs steeply to the large and prosperous stone-built village of **GHANDRUNG**.

Leave Ghandrung by a switchback of a trail, over a pass and down to cross a deep tributary valley, the Kimrong Khola, and from there climb steeply again to join another trail (the route from Ghorapani and Tadopani outlined below) leading to **TAGLUNG** and **CHHOMRONG** at the entrance to the Modi Khola's gorge where all Sanctuary-bound treks converge.

2) Ghorapani to Chhomrong; via Tadopani (1-2 days)

This is the route to choose if you have been tackling the Annapurna Circuit and wish to visit the Sanctuary on your way out to Pokhara. The trail to choose departs the main Muktinath-Pokhara route at **GHORAPANI DEURALI** and follows the ridge on the eastern side of the pass, enjoying views as grand as those from Poon Hill. It drops to a second pass (also **DEURALI**) with a lodge or two, and is joined by another optional trail coming from Chitre. A steep descent leads from Deurali to **BANTHANTI**, then switchbacks to the viewpoint of **TADOPANI**. Again a choice of route is offered. One descends to **GHANDRUNG**, while the other descends a little farther to the east, steeply into the valley of the Kimrong Khola, and climbs out on the opposite side for a long belvedere trail that leads directly to

CHHOMRONG.

To make a two-day approach it is advisable to spend the night in Tadapani.

RETURN ROUTES TO POKHARA

All routes out of the Annapurna Sanctuary necessarily retrace the inward trek as far as Chhomrong (two days), but from there a choice of trails become feasible. These are outlined below. Each alternative route is well-supplied with lodge accommodation and tea-houses.

1) Chhomrong to Pokhara; direct route via Landrung. (2-3 days)

This retraces the main trek described above, and is a little less strenuous than the way in. From **CHHOMRONG** follow the main path to the trail junction at **TAGLUNG**; bear left and descend steeply to **JINU** and continue all the way to **NEW BRIDGE**. Across the Modi Khola bear right and wander down-valley before rising on a clear trail as far as **LANDRUNG** (Landruk).

Climb out of Landrung and follow the well-trodden path through **BERI KHARKA** and over the ridge at **DEURALI**. Descend to **POTHANA** and **DHAMPUS**. If your plan is to walk all the way to Pokhara, spend a night here, then descend to the valley of the Yamdi Khola, go up to **NAUDANDA**, along the ridge towards Sarangkot and then descend to the lake at **POKHARA**. Alternatively, if you need to get to Pokhara quickly, do not stay in Dhampus but continue from it and make the descent to the Yamdi Khola near **SUIKHET** where it is possible to take a taxi or bus to **POKHARA**.

2) Chhomrong to Pokhara; via Ghandrung and Chandrakot. (2-3 days)

From **CHHOMRONG** walk along the main trail to the junction at **TAGLUNG**, but instead of descending by the left-hand fork, continue ahead, winding along the high path. This leads to another trail junction where you descend steeply through oak forest to the Kimrong

Machhapuchhare from Annapurna Base Camp (Sanctuary Stage 5)

Dhaulagiri at dawn from Poon Hill (Pilgrim Trail. Stage 3)
The Nilgiri Peaks across the Thak Khola from Tukuche (Pilgrim Trail. Stage 6)

Khola. The climb on the southern side is equally as steep. It crosses a ridge and in due course brings you to the important village of **GHANDRUNG**.

There is another major junction at Ghandrung, for one alternative route climbs to Ghorapani by way of Tadapani. Another descends to the Modi Khola and climbs on the eastern side to Landrung. The trail to Pokhara, however, heads south-west to **CHANDRAKOT**, crossing the Modi Khola on the way (or to Chandrakot via **BIRETHANTI** along the right bank of the river). From Chandrakot follow the outward route described at the end of the Annapurna Circuit trek via **NAUDANDA** and either **SUIKHET** or **SARANGKOT** to **POKHARA**.

3) Chhomrong to Pokhara; via Ghorapani. (4-5 days)

By using this route an interesting and visually rewarding circuit may be achieved. It is very strenuous in places, with much height gain and loss, but the effort is more than paid for by the views from Tadopani and Ghorapani.

Follow the route outlined above under option 2 as far as **GHANDRUNG**. Then, instead of continuing to Chandrakot, climb steeply to **TADOPANI**, a ridge-top settlement which gazes to Annapurna South, Hiunchuli and Machhapuchhare. From here cross the ridge and switchback through **BANTHANTI**, continue steeply again up to **DEURALI** and along a rhododendron-covered ridge to **GHORAPANI**. From **POON HILL** above Ghorapani the sunset and sunrise views of Dhaulagiri and the Annapurnas are legendary.

Leaving Ghorapani head south to **BIRETHANTI** as described at the end of the Annapurna Circuit details above. The continuing trail to Pokhara is also described thereafter, leading by way of **CHANDRAKOT**, **LUMLE**, **NAUDANDA** and **SARANGKOT**. A fine circuit.

THE PILGRIM'S TRAIL TO MUKTINATH

This world is but a thoroughfare full of woe,
And we being pilgrims passing to and fro. (Geoffrey Chaucer)

Unlike that of Chaucer's knight, the thoroughfare of the Pilgrim's Trail which leads from Pokhara to Muktinath, though steep at times, is far from being one of woe. Instead it is a constant evolution of delights, and pilgrims of both the Hindu and Buddhist faiths who tread it do so in a spirit of calm expectation. As might we. It is a trail that has been known for centuries (it is thought that pilgrims were drawn through the valley of the Kali Gandaki to Muktinath as early as 300 BC), and the greater part of it is that which generations of traders have used whilst journeying to and from Mustang and Tibet. This trade largely consisted of rice and barley from the lowlands of Nepal being carried north to Tibet, with Tibetan salt and wool being brought back down-valley.

The Pilgrim's Trail follows the Kali Gandaki upstream through the world's deepest valley, passing from the lush fertility of the middle hills to the stark and arid hillsides on the northern side of the Annapurna Himal - in the rain-shadow of the mountains.

It is probably the busiest of all trails in Nepal. In addition to Western trekkers and their entourage of guides and porters embarked upon this and the Annapurna Circuit which shares it, there are the long strings of pack animals that continue to carry goods from one end of the valley to the other - though since the Chinese invasion, no longer crossing into Tibet. There are the heavily-laden porters who keep the lodges and tea-houses stocked with goods, local Nepalis about their everyday business and, of course, the pilgrims for whom Muktinath is a holy site, one of the most important Hindu sites in the country.

From Pokhara to Muktinath and back will demand at least two weeks, but there is a possibility of shortening the return by flying out of Jomosom - although the availability of flights depends very much on stable weather conditions.

Features of the trek are the stupendous mountain views, of course. But in addition there are the dramatic contrasts of vegetation from one end of the valley to the other: climatic, architectural and cultural variations and a sense of shrugging off one world in exchange for a very different one on the northern side of the Himalayan Divide - "beyond the last blue mountain".

It's a trek equally suited to tea-house trekkers as it is to parties of campers. The Thakalis who inhabit much of the region through which the trek passes are noted hoteliers and their mountain lodges are among the finest in Nepal. Lodges and tea-houses are liberally scattered along the route, so independent trekkers can rely on frequent refreshment stops and accommodation all the way, and therefore travel light.

The maximum altitude this trek reaches is quite modest for Nepal too, for Muktinath stands at only 3802 metres (12,474ft) and as it is gained steadily over a number of days, altitude sickness should not be a problem. But even so, as Pokhara lies at less than 900 metres (3000ft), the overall height gain would appear sufficient to add spice.

In effect this route reverses the second half of the Annapurna Circuit. It begins in the low-lying Pokhara valley, rises to the ridge of the Kaski Danda above the Yamdi Khola and heads roughly north-westward to meet the Modi Khola which drains the Annapurna Sanctuary. Along this ridge magnificent views gaze off to the snow peaks that rim the Sanctuary, but after Chandrakot a steep descent is made to the Modi Khola, followed by a long and tiring climb to Ghorapani and the Poon Hill Danda: a substantial crest of rhododendron forest whose flanks are immaculately terraced for agriculture.

From Ghorapani a full day's descent leads into the valley of the Kali Gandaki overlooked first by Dhaulagiri and then by the shapely Nilgiri South whose coronet of peaks give this outlier of the Annapurnas a charisma all its own. Tatopani, the village of hot springs and gastronomic delights, is the main focus of trekkers in this part of the valley.

Beyond Tatopani the Pilgrim's Trail heads upvalley all the way; sometimes on the left bank, sometimes on the right, the big mountains soaring to unguessable heights above the river. Two days after

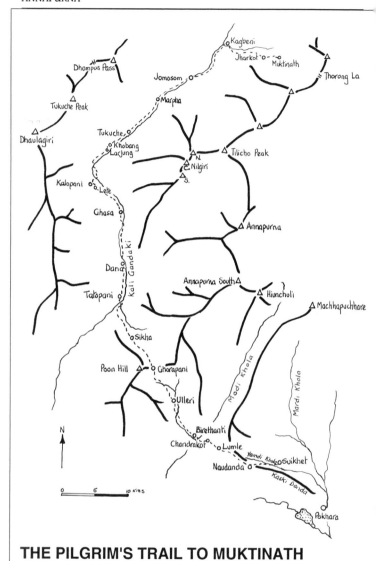

THE PILGRIM'S TRAIL TO MUKTINATH

ROUTE PROFILE:
THE PILGRIM'S TRAIL TO MUKTINATH

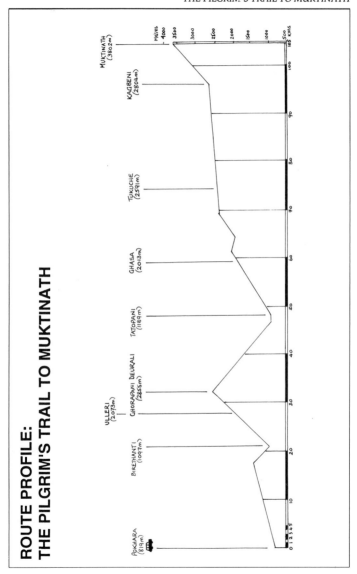

133

leaving Tatopani you pass immediately below Dhaulagiri and then head north-eastwards. Here the valley is broad, its bed stony, the river (known in these upper reaches as the Thak Khola) making its anarchistic way in numerous braidings. Villages are particularly attractive: Khobang, Tukuche, Marpha - each one giving witness to the Nilgiri peaks opposite, and to Dhaulagiri high above. Annapurna itself is out of sight, hidden by the Nilgiris.

An easy walk beyond Marpha brings you to Jomosom, the administrative centre of the valley, and above this busy little town a choice of routes are on offer for the final day to Muktinath. One trail visits the medieval village of Kagbeni in the valley bed, the other climbs round a spur of mountain and ascends gradually to handsome Jharkot and finally, to Muktinath itself.

It's a fine trek, perhaps the least demanding in this book, but no less worthy for all that.

STAGE 1:
POKHARA - LUMLE - BIRETHANTI

Distance:	24 kilometres (15 miles) overall
Time:	5$\frac{1}{2}$-6 hours (with transport to Suikhet)
Start altitude:	819m (2687ft)
High point:	Khare 1737m (5699ft)
Height gain:	918m (3012ft)
Descent:	640m (2100ft)
Accommodation:	Lodges in Naudanda, Khare, Lumle, Chandrakot and Birethanti
Transport options:	Bus or taxi (Pokhara-Suikhet) It may also be possible to arrange transport as far as Lumle.

The following stage has been written with the assumption that you will take advantage of the road which now runs from Pokhara through the valley of the Yamdi Khola. This road is planned to continue eventually as far as Baglung in the lower reaches of the Kali Gandaki between Beni and Kusma. At the time of writing it goes through Naudanda and on beyond Lumle. Transport is readily available as far as Suikhet, but beyond that the road is open only to construction traffic. However, trekkers are known to have obtained lifts to Lumle in the trucks that ply to and fro. If you choose this option you run the risk if getting covered with a film of white dust. By the time this book is published, of course, it may be possible to ride a bus or taxi as far as Lumle, in which case walking time from there to Birethanti will be in the region of two hours.

Times quoted for this stage of the walk are based on the trek beginning at Suikhet. The bus to Suikhet leaves from Bagar, near the Shining Hospital in Pokhara.

It is possible, of course, to shun transport and walk all the way from Pokhara. In this case either follow the trail which leads from the northern shore of the Phewa lake up to the ridge of the Kaski Danda, or take a trail heading from near the Shining Hospital up the eastern end of the same ridge to Sarangkot. A good path then winds along the ridge to reach Naudanda. If you decide to adopt this route, allow an extra half-day for the overall trek.

As the first stage of the long walk to Muktinath trekkers may need reminding that it will be necessary to show trek permits at the various check posts along the trail. The first of these is in Naudanda, a long, straggling village on the ridge of the Kaski Danda from where there are lovely views to the snow-crest of the Annapurna-Lamjung Himal rising in the north. Views from here are particularly fine in the early morning and evening. In fact views are delightful throughout the walk to Chandrakot at the western end of the ridge, making a magnificent scenic introduction to the region despite the road's intrusion.

Solo trekkers are advised to find company for the first few days on the trail, since the route passes through a region with an unfortunate reputation for muggings. Even those travelling in a group should take precautions during an overnight camp a day or two from the road, and it is usual for parties of campers to have a Sherpa on guard overnight in case of theft from tents. Happily such incidents are still a rarity in Nepal, but an awareness of the problem will help to combat it.

The bus from Pokhara to Suikhet takes a little under an hour, while private taxi will be somewhat quicker. From Suikhet wander to Phedi at the foot of the hill to the south and take the clear trail which climbs the left-hand hillside through woodland, leap-frogging the road to reach **NAUDANDA** (1425m: 4675ft 1¹/₂hrs *accommodation,* *refreshments*). The road also passes through the village, a fact which has the effect of detracting from its former charm.

Follow the crest of the ridge westwards on a trail that is soon rejoined by the road. For much of the way to Lumle walk along the road, but take footpath short-cuts where possible. In about an hour and a half from Naudanda reach **KHARE** (1737m: 5699ft 3hrs *accommodation, refreshments*), a village situated in a pass at the head of the Yamdi Khola. An alternative route cuts off northwards from here and is useful for trekkers heading for the Sanctuary. Our route, however, continues ahead, passes a British-run farming project which gives ex-Gurkha soldiers training in agricultural management, and then enters **LUMLE** (1615m: 5299ft 3hrs 45mins *accommodation, refreshments*). On the road a sign announces "Beginning of Trekking".

Lumle is a pleasant, traditional village whose main street is paved with stone slabs. There are several lodges, but unless you have a special reason to stay here it would be better to continue at least as far as Chandrakot before stopping for the night.

This village is reached in another half-hour by a trail that goes along the side of the ridge. **CHANDRAKOT** (1600m: 5249ft 4hrs 15mins *accommodation, refreshments*) sits at the very end of the ridge overlooking the valley of the Modi Khola. It has some classic views to enjoy, especially to Annapurna South and Machhapuchhare marking the entrance to the Annapurna Sanctuary.

The descent to Birethanti is a steep one. It takes you down to the Modi Khola on stone steps, then follows the river downstream to a suspension bridge. Cross this and enter **BIRETHANTI** (1097m: 3599ft) which sits at the confluence of the Modi Khola and Bhurungdi Khola, an obvious place to stay for the night before addressing the long haul towards Ghorapani. There is a police check post here, a number of lodges, shops and even a bank. Upstream of the village a pool in the Bhurungdi river is tempting to laze in after a dusty day's walk.

STAGE 2:
BIRETHANTI - ULLERI

Distance:	**7 kilometres (4 miles)**
Time:	**4-4½ hours**
Start altitude:	**1097m (3599ft)**
High point:	**Ulleri 2073m (6801ft)**
Height gain:	**976m (3202ft)**
Accommodation:	**Lodges in Hille, Tirkhedunga and Ulleri**

The climb to Ghorapani Deurali from the banks of the Modi Khola is remorseless, gaining more than 1700 metres (5500ft) in height. It is therefore worth breaking it into two separate stages, and since Ulleri is reached after a tiring ascent of thousands of stone steps, it seems an obvious place to stop. Actually, taken slowly the climb will be achieved without too much pain, although on a warm day laden trekkers are bound to lose a litre or two of moisture.

Despite the effort involved there is plenty to enjoy: the pleasures of cultivated hillsides, distant mountain views and the busy daily life of both the trail and the settlements you pass through. Tea-houses are situated with some frequency along the pathway, which does away with the need to carry flasks of liquid.

Wander through Birethanti and follow the north bank of the Bhurungdi Khola, initially in the shade of bamboo forest, and pass a picturesque waterfall. Ignore a sturdy-looking suspension bridge over the river and continue on its north bank (true left side), steadily rising now through two settlements and cultivated farmland to reach **HILLE** (1524m: 5000ft 2hrs *accommodation, refreshments*), a village with several lodges. Ten minutes or so further along the trail lies **TIRKHEDUNGA** (1577m: 5174ft 2hrs 15mins *accommodation, refreshments*), some of whose lodges are advertised as being run by ex-Gurkha soldiers.

Outside Tirkhedunga cross left onto a suspension bridge over a stream, then go over the Bhurungdi Khola before tackling the long staircase of stone steps (nearly 4000 of them) that lead to Ulleri. Tea-houses offer welcome refreshment along the way, and as you gain height so views to the big peaks rising in the east help take your mind off the ascent.

Two hours or so from Tirkhedunga brings you to **ULLERI** (2073m: 6801ft). This straggling, slate-roofed Magar village makes a pleasant and attractive overnight resting place. From it you gaze deeply into the valley of the Bhurungdi Khola and out towards Pokhara, the way you have come. There are plenty of lodges, both in the village itself and a little above it.

STAGE 3:

ULLERI - GHORAPANI

Distance:	**5 kilometres (3 miles)**
Time:	**3-3¹/₂ hours**
Start altitude:	**2073m (6801ft)**
High point:	**Ghorapani Deurali 2855m (9367ft)**
Height gain:	**782m (2566ft)**
Accommodation:	**Lodges in Banthanti, Nyathanti, Ghorapani and Ghorapani Deurali**

An easier, less severe stage than yesterday's, the climb to Ghorapani passes mostly through forests of oak and rhododendron, so views are restricted. The warning about not walking alone here is repeated. Mostly, of course, the trail will be busy with other trekkers, porters and, possibly, strings of pack animals working their way to or from the upper villages of the Thak Khola, or even Mustang. These pack horses have bells jingling at their necks, and the lead animals are often brightly caparisoned with colourful plumes or, less exotically as has been seen recently, with streamers consisting of recording tape unravelled from a trekker's walkman cassette!

Keen bird watchers should enjoy this stage. Nepal boasts an impressive bird count and more than 440 species have been recorded within the Annapurna region. The grey langur also inhabits the forests either side of Ghorapani's ridge and may be seen swinging through the trees above the trail.

Above Ulleri the trail climbs steadily through farmland, but before long you enter forest again and in about an hour arrive in the settlement of **BANTHANTI** (2307m: 7569ft *accommodation,*

Annapurna I, Annapurna South and Hiunchuli - from Poon Hill

refreshments). Crossing one or two streams the way climbs on and reaches **NYATHANTI** (2606m: 8550ft 2$^{1}/_{2}$hrs *accommodation, refreshments*), a collection of lodges in a forest clearing.

The majority of the stage is already over, for there are only another 250 metres to climb before coming onto the ridge at Ghorapani Deurali. **GHORAPANI** (2819m: 9249ft 3hrs *accommodation, refreshments*) is reached soon after. This is the original settlement, built before the demand for accommodation for trekkers turned the pass above into a resort of lodges and tea-houses. Ghorapani is a rather haphazard collection of lodges and houses in a much-denuded patch of forest. Another ten minutes or so uphill on the stone-slab trail will bring you to the growing number of trekkers' lodges crowded atop the pass on the Poon Hill Danda known here as **GHORAPANI DEURALI** (2855m: 9367ft). The police check post is situated beside the trail at the southern end of the village.

Whilst staying overnight here make a point of going up onto Poon Hill itself (3198m: 10,492ft), the crown of hill to the left (west) of Deurali, to enjoy magnificent views of Annapurna South, Hiunchuli and Machhapuchhare to the north-east, and to the great mass of Dhaulagiri hovering to the north. Sunset and sunrise views from this belvedere are outstanding. It is reached in a little over half an hour from the centre of Ghorapani Deurali. Signposts indicate the start of the path to it.

STAGE 4:

GHORAPANI - SIKHA - TATOPANI

Distance:	**14 kilometres (8$^{1}/_{2}$ miles)**
Time:	**4$^{1}/_{2}$-5 hours**
Start altitude:	**2855m (9367ft)**
Low point:	**Ghar Khola 1173m (3848ft)**
Descent:	**1682m (5519ft)**
Accommodation:	**Chitre, Phalante, Sikha, Ghara and Tatopani**

This is a beautiful day's walk. After the visual restrictions imposed by forest on the southern side of the Poon Hill Danda it is a delight to be wandering downhill with open views ahead. Dhaulagiri dominates the northern horizon: a great block of mountain draped with snow and ice. Below it the shadowed defile of the Kali Gandaki's valley is but a hint for much of the way, but as you descend to it, so the well-crafted profile of Nilgiri South rises from the valley to add a new dimension. Before the Kali Gandaki is the Ghar Khola, the tributary valley into which drain most of the hillsides of our descent.

By far the majority of this descent is through hillsides terraced with an intricate pattern of fields and with groups of trees and shrubs casting reservoirs of shade upon them. There are several villages lining the route; isolated tea-houses, individual homes and grain stores. The pathway is stepped. In one or two places there are landslip areas to cross. There are paved trails through the villages, and plenty of chautaara (porter's resting places), both in the open and in the shade of pipal trees. And the trail is a-bustle with activity.

Descend initially through rhododendron forest on the northern side of the Poon Hill Danda. The trail is likely to be muddy here, churned as it is by the hooves of countless pack animals, but as you emerge below the forest so the way improves.

CHITRE (2316m: 7598ft *accommodation, refreshments*) is the first village met on the descent. It's a scattered settlement with a few

Terraces below the Durkun Danda

lodges and tea-houses, and an alternative trail that breaks off to the right, cutting back to cross the ridge east of Ghorapani. Ignore this and continue on the main trail and soon after come to **PHALANTE** (2256m: 7402ft *accommodation, refreshments*), a small village with a couple of lodges and a school.

Both above and below Sikha the trail crosses patches of hillside regularly cut by landslides where the path will no doubt be temporary only, for it is likely to be washed away with the next monsoon - another export from Nepal to the lowlands of the Indian sub-continent far away to the south.

SIKHA (1920m: 6299ft 2hrs *accommodation, refreshments*) is the largest village between Ghorapani and Tatopani. Built on a series of different levels it has a number of simple lodges, tea-houses and shops, and exploits a wonderful vista with (1) Dhaulagiri demanding attention: an arctic world lodged in the sky high above a foreground of cultivated terraces. The upper part of Sikha lines a secondary ridge below which the rest of its houses huddle beside the stone-paved trail.

Below Sikha the path winds on, skirting the terraces, and comes to another village. **GHARA** (1768m: 5801ft 2¹/₂hrs *accommodation, refreshments*) is a busy place with one or two shops in addition to its lodges. Again, views of Dhaulagiri are quite magical from here.

The ridge of the Durkun Danda has to be crossed for the final descent to the Ghar Khola's confluence with the Kali Gandaki. On the way to it you go through a small settlement, but on the ridge itself, in a dip through which the trail passes, a tea-house stands at a point known as **SANTOSH HILL** *(refreshments)*. From this point you gaze down onto the forests that clothe the lower slopes, and then descend into them. Far below can be seen the first glimmer of the Kali Gandaki.

More stone-paved steps lead down past several tea-houses. At the foot of the stairway join another trail and bear left, and soon after come to a group of buildings (3hrs 45mins *refreshments*) on the left bank of the Kali Gandaki. There is a junction of trails. The left-hand option leads alongside the river heading downstream and goes to Beni. We bear right, however, cross a bridge over the **GHAR KHOLA** (1173m: 3848ft), go through the small village named after it, and then cross a long suspension bridge to the west bank of the Kali Gandaki, with a superb view upvalley towards Nilgiri South. The trail then heads upstream on a modest switchback and soon reaches **TATOPANI** (1189m: 3901ft). A police check post is found at the southern end of the main street and you should show your trek permit there.

Tatopani nestles in almost the lowest part of the valley through which the trek will lead. High above, the Kali Gandaki is walled by the two monstrous massifs of Dhaulagiri and Annapurna; at this point their summits rise more than 6900 metres (22,600ft) over the village.

Tatopani has been popular with trekkers virtually since trekking began in Nepal. It's a busy, bustling community whose paved street is lined with lodges, shops, post office and restaurants, some of which overlook the river, others that have tables set out in gardens among orange or banana trees. It is very much the gastronomic centre of trekking in the Annapurna region, and the variety of delicacies offered on restaurant menus is quite astonishing. Tatopani is also known, of course, for its hot springs (the name means "hot water") down at the riverside. (If you decide to take advantage of these springs, please do not use soap in the hot water pools.)

Points of Interest Along the Way:

1: DHAULAGIRI (8167m: 26,795ft) is the world's seventh highest summit, a huge, graceful peak whose name rather aptly means "white mountain". The first Westerner to see it close-to was the Swiss geologist, Arnold Heim, who flew through the valley in a Dakota in 1949. The following year Maurice Herzog led an experienced team from France on an attempt to find a way to the summit, but detailed reconnaissance failed to locate a justifiable route. In the ensuing years six further expeditions made attempts to climb the mountain, but it was not until 1960 that a Swiss team actually achieved success - but only after they had been airlifted onto the North-east Col at 5877 metres (19,281ft).

STAGE 5:

TATOPANI - DANA - GHASA

Distance:	**12 kilometres (7¹⁄₂ miles)**
Time:	**4¹⁄₂-5 hours**
Start altitude:	**1189m (3901ft)**
High point:	**Ghasa 2013m (6604ft)**
Height gain:	**824m (2703ft)**
Accommodation:	**Lodges in Dana, Kopchepani, Pairothapla and Ghasa**

On this stage of the trek the landscape grows wilder and more alpine. Heading north towards the Himalayan Divide you turn your back to the sub-tropical vegetation of the middle hills and wander into a rugged countryside where terraced fields are rare, deciduous trees mostly give way to conifers and the architecture of village houses reflects a changing climate.

Although the amount of height gain is rather modest on this stage, there is a certain amount of roller-coasting on the trail to confuse the figures. Above Dana the route is often located on the western side of the valley, but severe landslides had created a diversion to the east bank when the route was being surveyed. Whether the trail will be remade on the left bank is unsure. Enquire of other trekkers or locals before you leave Dana itself. Should it be re-routed along the west bank of the river the trail will not take you through either Kopchepani or Pairothapla.

The continuing route out of Tatopani is in full view of the soaring face of Nilgiri South (6839m: 22,438ft), one of the western outliers of the Annapurna massif. It lures you on for some way, but later Dhaulagiri takes command of the valley. Across the river a short distance from Tatopani a tributary valley provides an enticing view of the upper ice walls of the Annapurna massif, a promise of things to come.

Follow the trail upvalley, passing groves of orange trees and keeping to the west side as far as Dana. A short distance beyond Tatopani you pass through the settlement of **GUITE** *(refreshments)* where there is a suspension bridge over the Kali Gandaki. Ignore this and continue with the river on your right, cross a bridge over a side-stream, walk through **SUKE BAGAR** and shortly after arrive in the first part of **DANA** (1446m: 4744ft 1hr 15mins *accommodation, refreshments*), a large and prosperous village built in three distinct sections. The lower and middle parts have lodge accommodation, while the middle and upper thirds are separated by a tributary stream draining through a broad and stony bed. The last of Dana's three parts has some large three-storey buildings with intricately carved windows. Dana has shops, a post office and a police check post.

As outlined in the introduction to this stage of the trek, the continuing route upvalley is subject to landslides and whilst the trail crossed to the east (true left) bank during research for this guidebook, it could be that the west bank route is open again in the near future. Check for up-to-date information before leaving Dana. On the northern edge of the village a rather rickety wooden bridge crosses to the east bank. (There was another bridge upstream near the village of Rupse Chhaharo, but this was out of use late in 1991 and the only possible route upvalley necessitated crossing the bridge at Dana. Follow local advice.)

Once across this bridge head upvalley, go through a small settlement and follow the trail as it climbs over a high shoulder of hillside; fine views are enjoyed from here, not just back downvalley, but across to Rupse Chhaharo and its waterfalls. At the high point you pass two or three houses then descend quite steeply to the edge of **KOPCHEPANI** (1676m: 5499ft $2^{1}/_{2}$hrs *accommodation, refreshments*). Continue upvalley, now climbing again, steeply in places, on a rough and rocky trail. Pass more tea-houses and then reach **PAIROTHAPLA** (1951m: 6401ft 3¹/₂hrs *accommodation, refreshments*), a small settlement with a trekkers' lodge and rather basic shop.

With a few switchbacks high above the river the way now passes through the narrows of a gorge, descends to a suspension bridge (4hrs 15mins) and then recrosses to the west bank of the Kali Gandaki. About 15 minutes later reach the Thakali village of **GHASA** (2013m: 6604ft).

Like Dana, Ghasa is also a three-part village, each section of which has accommodation. The middle section is best. The street is paved and there is a stream running through. There are lodges, a nearby waterfall and teasing views upvalley. Some of Ghasa's flat-roofed buildings stand on stilts, while others are of a more solid stone construction.

STAGE 6:

GHASA - TUKUCHE

Distance:	15 kilometres (9 miles)
Time:	5¹/₂ hours
Start altitude:	2013m (6604ft)
High point:	Tukuche 2591m (8501ft)
Height gain:	578m (1897ft)
Accommodation:	Lodges in Lete, Kalopani, Larjung, Khobang and Tukuche

This is a delightful, ever-interesting day's trek, in which you pass between the giants of Dhaulagiri and Annapurna to enter the upper part of the valley, known locally as Thak Khola. The area receives much less rainfall than the lower reaches of the Kali Gandaki and this, together with the increased altitude, has an obvious affect on vegetation. Much of it now is alpine with pinewoods dominating, but there are also willow groves and orchards too, bearing fruit in the shadow of the mountains.

Above Kalopani the valley makes a determined sweep to the right (north-east) and views become truly dramatic. Huge mountains rise on either side, and glaciers and high snowfields contrast the somewhat arid, stony wastes of the valley bed. There's a broad tributary valley to cross with no bridge to aid you; there will then be several braided streams to leap or, possibly, to wade through.

The very nature of the trek enters a new phase. After Lete there are few steep climbs to be made, and once you round the curve of the valley above Koketani, the Thak Khola draws you into a series of strange new landscapes that will culminate with the colouring and textures of Tibet on the hillsides between Kagbeni and Muktinath in two days' time. Between Ghasa and Muktinath there are some of the most delightful villages of the whole Pilgrim's Trail. On this stage there's Khobang with its covered walkway, and historic Tukuche at the end of the day, with several fine lodges.

Leaving Ghasa the trail soon makes an undulating course along the steep hillsides that form the western wall of the valley. There is a landslip area to cross, then you descend some stone steps and arrive at a suspension bridge over the Lete Khola. Across the bridge stands the **NAMASTE LODGE** (1½hrs *accommodation, refreshments*). From it a steep ascent is made of a hillside spur jutting between the Lete Khola and the Kali Gandaki. At the top of the climb pass through a stand of pines and enter **LETE** (2438m: 7999ft 2hrs *accommodation, refreshments*).

Lete is another long straggling village and it's difficult to know where it ends and Kalopani begins. Towards the northern end there is a police check post and a number of Western-style buildings. Dhaulagiri is seen almost directly ahead, while (1) Annapurna I rises in the east. From here the evening alpenglow on Annapurna is quite beautiful. An alternative trail on the opposite bank of the river crosses a ridge and heads up to the base camp area used by Herzog's successful expedition in 1950. This makes a demanding trek without either tea-houses or lodges.

Walk through Lete and into **KALOPANI** (2530m: 8301ft 2hrs 15mins *accommodation, refreshments*), and about 10 minutes later reach a suspension bridge over the Kali Gandaki. Cross to the east bank and continue along the path heading upvalley. It's an easy, gentle trail that leads past **DHAMPU** a (few minutes beyond the bridge and, half an hour later, comes to **KOKETANI** (3hrs 15mins *refreshments*).

Beyond Koketani climb round the left-hand side of a pine-covered bluff and descend to a long suspension bridge that once more returns you to the true right bank of the Kali Gandaki, now on its northern side. Bear right and a few moments later descend into the bed of the Ghatte Khola, a major tributary that drains out of a vast amphitheatre formed by the east-facing walls of the Dhaulagiri massif. Gazing into this amphitheatre, Dhaulagiri is the peak high to the left (but severely foreshortened), the North-east Col is in the centre, and to the right of that the ridge climbs to Tukuche Peak (6920m: 22,703ft). Generations of Thakali shepherds have taken their flocks to graze in the high meadows below the glaciers, and their trails may be used by trekkers today seeking an interesting diversion from the main route. If you are tempted to try this, food and tents will need to be carried, and you should not stray too near the hanging glaciers as collapsing seracs constitute a very real danger.

Continuing on the Pilgrim's Trail cross the bed of the Ghatte Khola to the far side. There is no major trail across, but you will no doubt be able to see vague paths made by porters and previous trekkers. The Ghatte Khola consists of a series of streams and rivulets. As there is no permanent bridge you must either wade these various streams or use whatever aids have been put there (stepping stones or temporary log "bridges"). A walking stick will be helpful in maintaining balance.

Once over follow the continuing trail as it climbs up and down along the left-hand hillside among pinewoods. Out of the trees lovely views across the valley show the three Nilgiri peaks (North, Central and South) effectively blocking the way to Annapurna. In a little over an hour from Koketani come to **LARJUNG** (2550m: 8366ft 4hrs 15mins *accommodation, refreshments*) which almost merges with Khobang. The lodges here stand at the entrance to the village.

Pass through Larjung, cross a stream by way of a wooden bridge and shortly after enter the charming village of **KHOBANG** (2560m: 8399ft 4 1/2 hrs *accommodation, refreshments*). The way through Khobang passes along a central tunnel from which access is made to local houses, thus protecting them from the strong winds that gust through the valley on most days. Trekkers with high backpacks may need to duck low in places to avoid catching them on large wooden beams. The village has an important Buddhist *gompa*, the first of several to be found in this part of the valley.

From here to Kagbeni the Thak Khola is regularly swept by strong southerly winds that usually start to blow during the late morning and last for most of the day. Whilst you may experience dust, sand and even small stones being blown into your back on the walk, the worst effects of these winds will be felt, of course, on the return downvalley as you face into them.

Out of Khobang you can either choose to continue upvalley along the trail which hugs the left-hand slope, or walk in the stony bed of the valley itself. If you choose the latter course there will be a few modest winding streams to leap, but during the main trekking seasons these should create no real problems.

About one hour from Khobang arrive in (2) **TUKUCHE** (2591m: 8501ft), a large and important village in two sections divided by an open flat meadow where Nepali traders used to meet their counterparts from Tibet in order to conduct business. There is accommodation to be found in both sections of the village, the larger selection of lodges being located in the southern part.

Points of Interest Along the Way:

1: ANNAPURNA (8091m: 26,545ft) was, of course, the first 8000 metre peak to be climbed. The successful French expedition, under the leadership of Maurice Herzog, originally came to Nepal in the spring of 1950 with the aim of making an attempt on Dhaulagiri. From a base at Tukuche they undertook extensive reconnaissance outings before deciding that Dhaulagiri was not for them, and decided instead to focus their attentions on Annapurna. But first they had to find it. In the course of their explorations team members crossed the Tilicho La and descended to Manang in the Marsyangdi valley, then returned confused to Tukuche. Back down-valley they found access to the north side of Annapurna by way of the Miristi Khola. With the unsettled conditions of the monsoon just arriving, the summit was reached by Herzog and Louis Lachenal on 3 June 1950. On the descent they were forced to bivouac in a crevasse and, both suffering severe frostbite, had to fight their way to safety amid constant storms. Their retreat from the mountain is one of the most harrowing tales in mountaineering's history, and is told in Herzog's classic book, *Annapurna*.

2: TUKUCHE is a typical Thakali village with some striking-looking buildings, several of which display the skills of the wood carver on doorways and round windows. However, since its important trading links with Tibet ceased with the Chinese invasion of the 1950s, the village lost its most important source of income and today some of the back street houses show signs of decay and abandonment where villagers deserted the valley and went off to Pokhara or into the Terai to start new businesses. Some of these villagers retained their properties, though, and return to spend holidays with family and friends in Tukuche. With the increase in trekking, and the demand for food and accommodation, some of that financial loss has now been regained, as is evident from the improvements made to some of the lodges in recent times.

Tukuche's orchards provide abundant fresh fruit in the autumn which is used, not only in lodge meals, but also in a local form of *rakshi*, and at certain times home-grown apples may be bought at very low prices. As with other villages in this part of the Thak Khola, Tukuche has electricity, thanks to a small-scale hydro scheme down-valley.

Experienced trekkers with time to spare could make an interesting, but demanding, side trip from here (or from Marpha, which has an alternative trail) up the steep northern hillside to the Dhampus Pass (5250m: 17,224ft) located high on a ridge between Tukuche Peak and Thapa Peak. (A minimum of two days will be required to get from Tukuche to the pass.) Over the pass it would be possible for strong and experienced parties with the necessary equipment to descend into the upper end of Hidden Valley, then cross French Pass (glaciated) down to the Myagdi Khola for a circuit of Dhaulagiri. Camping equipment and food for many days would need to be carried. (The Dhaulagiri Inner Circuit is briefly outlined - in a clockwise direction - in the chapter headed: *Other Trek Ideas*.)

STAGE 7:
TUKUCHE - JOMOSOM - KAGBENI

Distance:	**20 kilometres (12$\frac{1}{2}$ miles)**
Time:	**5 hours**
Start altitude:	**2591m (8501ft)**
High point:	**Kagbeni 2804m (9199ft)**
Height gain:	**213m (698ft)**
Accommodation:	**Lodges in Marpha, Jomosom, Eklebhatti and Kagbeni**

Moving on from Tukuche you pass right into the rain-shadow of the mountains where you have a veiled hint of the mysterious, once-forbidden kingdom of Mustang. There is little height to be gained on this stage of the trek. The river which you follow exploits a broad swathe through the mountains, but its bed has risen with the Himalayan uplift and since its early tributaries have little rain-borne power it does not have a strong carving effect here. It meanders through a wide and stony bed and it's only when it gathers the glacier-melt from Dhaulagiri and the Annapurnas that it develops the strength to scour a deeper trench on the outflow from the mountains. Here in the Thak Khola you wander through a high but mostly level valley with rare ease, and have time to enjoy the raw grandeur that is steadily revealed on either side.

Man's impact gives added interest. Marpha is a delightful village where the industrious nature of the Thakali people has inspired some admirable architecture and a drainage system unique in this part of the Himalaya. As the administrative centre for the Mustang District Jomosom is a busy town, but with a special atmosphere all its own, while Kagbeni belongs to another age: an age that bears little relationship with today.

Today's walk is a gem, a total contrast to the early stages of the trek just out of Pokhara. If you are travelling through the Thak Khola region in the autumn trekking season (October-December) you might be lucky enough to experience one of the colourful Buddhist festivals held at the monasteries (gompas) of Tukuche, Marpha or Syang. These dyokyapsi *are celebrations of masked dancing, a little like the well-known Mani Rimdu festival held in the Everest region of Solu Khumbu.*

Valley-bed cultivation near Marpha

It will take about an hour and a half to walk from Tukuche to Marpha. Along the trail you will have continued fine views to enjoy of the mountains on the opposite side of the valley, with Tilicho Peak coming into sight beyond Nilgiri North. Shortly before reaching the first village you pass the Marpha Agricultural Farm and its orchards.

MARPHA (2667m: 8750ft 1¹/₂hrs *accommodation, refreshments*) is an extremely attractive place with a narrow paved street under which the village drainage system runs. Lodges here are among the best in the Thak Khola. Some of them have inner courtyards where you can sit protected from the winds; others have partially-sheltered rooftop restaurants with magnificent views of the mountains rising in the east. Marpha has a post office and a library. Of its several shops there is one that advertises boot repairs - a point worth noting if you've trouble with your footwear, or the stitching on your rucksack.

Leave Marpha and pass through a *kani* (a decorated Buddhist construction that marks the entrance and exit to a village) and follow the clear trail as it heads upvalley among a few trees and shrubs. There are grand views down-valley to Dhaulagiri, and it is worth pausing now and then to enjoy them. On the approach to the next village, Syang, note the small terraced fields scraped over generations along the edge of the valley bed; a picture of ingenuity and determination to wrest a harvest from a harsh and uncompromising land.

SYANG is a small village with a *gompa* perched on the hill above. The trail winds below it and heads across the tributary of the Syang Khola where a wooden bridge spans the stream. Rising round a spur on a broad track you come into view of Jomosom, in the valley itself. It is an easy stroll along the track to it, following a line of electricity cables strung from wild-angled poles. Near the suspension bridge at the entrance there is a police check post where it is necessary to show your trek permit.

JOMOSOM (2713m: 8901ft 3hrs *accommodation, refreshments*) is a large, sprawling township that straddles the river. As the main town of the valley it is an important place, by far the largest habitation since leaving Pokhara. There are many lodges, shops, banks, administration buildings, a military post, hospital, post office and a STOL airstrip. Scheduled flights link Jomosom with Pokhara, but the weather (especially the wind) regularly plays havoc with the schedules and flights can be unreliable.

Remain on the west bank until the main trail swings round to cross the river by a bridge (not the suspension bridge as you enter), and continue upvalley through the village. Just beyond the military post on the outskirts of Jomosom the trail heads along the right-hand edge (east side) of the valley bed. It's a stony but sometimes sandy way, yet it is always easy and you can stride along with the wind at your back and make good progress. In places the trail undulates along the lower hillside, but mostly it takes you through the bed itself, crossing several minor streams as you go. And with each pace you tread deeper into a strange, but magical land. Among the stones that form the valley bed you may notice some curious, smooth black ones, known locally as (1) *shaligrams* which are sometimes used in worship by Hindus.

In an hour and a half from Jomosom you will come to a pair of isolated lodges snug against the foot of the eastern hillside. **EKLEBHATTI** (2758m: 9049ft 4¹/₂hrs *accommodation, refreshments*) actually means "lonely inn" and is the name now more commonly used than its original one of Chyancha Lhrenba. A trail found just beyond the buildings angles up the right-hand slope and heads off to Muktinath in about 3-3$^1/_2$ hours. This is the direct route, clear and easy. In just over an hour from Eklebhatti it joins the Kagbeni-Muktinath trail (described below) on a broad shelf of hillside.

From Eklebhatti continue ahead along the right-hand edge of the valley bed and in half an hour you will reach the willow-girt oasis of **KAGBENI** (2804m: 9199ft) at the confluence of the Jhang Khola and Thak Khola. It's a wonderful, fortress-like medieval place of narrow alleys, *chortens*, the remains of an old palace and a large fortified *gompa* overlooking all. There are several lodges within the village, and water mills outside. Kagbeni has a police check post, as befits a town which acts as the gateway to the ancient trading route that leads to Mustang and Tibet. All around rise dun-coloured hills, barely vegetated, arid and barren in the dry atmosphere that is more akin to that of the Tibetan Plain than of the rest of Nepal to the south.

Points of Interest Along the Way:

1: SHALIGRAMS are the strange smooth black stones found in the bed of the Thak Khola and in certain parts of the hills above. They contain fossilised sea creatures, or ammonites, that lived around a hundred million years or more ago in the Tethys Sea. This sea was lost when the Indian tectonic plate collided with that of the main land-mass of Asia; the collision that caused - and continues to cause - the uplifting of the Himalaya. These *shaligrams* have a religious significance for Hindus, for whom they represent several deities, and they will be found in many temples of the Hindu world. Along the trail between Marpha and Muktinath Tibetan traders will be seen offering *shaligrams* for sale.

STAGE 8:

KAGBENI - MUKTINATH

Distance:	**9 kilometres (5¹/2 miles)**
Time:	**3-3¹/2 hours**
Start altitude:	**2804m (9199ft)**
High point:	**Muktinath 3802m (12,474ft)**
Height gain:	**998m (3274ft)**
Accommodation:	**Jharkot and Muktinath (Ranipauwa)**

This final stage on the Pilgrim's Trail underlines impressions gained on the approach to Kagbeni: impressions of other-worldliness. So different are the landscapes on this northern side of the Himalayan Divide: so tantalisingly remote and evocative of a moonscape with the vast barren slopes, wind-eroded cliffs and, as you draw nearer to your goal, long-distant vistas in which the lofty ice-diamond mountains impress their personalities from afar.

The trail is a dusty one: broad on the lower slopes, but guided by irrigation channels or drystone walls towards Jharkot and Muktinath. A few scrawny trees defy the altitude and open pools of water that draw an evening skim of ice open by day to mirror the distant peaks. Pony trains and laden porters supply the last settlements with food that cannot be grown here. The eyes of Indian sadhus, scantily clad despite lingering snows, shine with prospects of reaching the summit of their pilgrimage; in some cases a pilgrimage that has taken months of hard journeying to complete.

It will be a day of wonder for all who trek here with eyes to see the riches of this remote world. Look beyond the aridity, beyond the parched hills and cliffs of erosion, and glory in this still-evolving, still-growing land. And absorb its magic and its mystery as you wander.

Cross the tributary of the Jhong Khola and follow the trail that climbs initially among terraces and then over bare, uncultivated hillsides heading east. The rise is steep in places for you gain about 350 metres (1100ft) in a little over an hour to join the main trail rising from the south - the direct route from Eklebhatti. Continue to rise, more steadily now, towards Muktinath. Off to your left is the deep cleft through which the Jhong Khola drains, its upper cliffs piped and pitted by wind erosion.

A few minutes walk below Muktinath stands the magical village of Jharkot

KHINGAR *(refreshments)* is the first village, but the trail skirts to the south of it. There is a tea-house beside the trail. **JHARKOT** (3612m: 11,850ft 2hrs 45mins *accommodation, refreshments*) is the next settlement, and what a delight this is. Partially fortified, like Kagbeni this too is a medieval village, but built on a spur of hillside and with a few small willow-fringed ponds lying below it and poplars and peach trees nearby.

The trail edges through Jharkot and resumes on a clear rise above it, for much of the way alongside an irrigation channel, and in another 45 minutes reaches the village of Muktinath, more properly known as Ranipauwa. Muktinath is the name of the religious site a few minutes above the village.

MUKTINATH (3802m: 12,474ft) has grown around a large rest house for pilgrims. It has many lodges, tea-houses and a few shops. There are several campsites too, and a police check post towards the upper end of the main thoroughfare. Tibetan traders squat in the street where they spread out their wares beneath the feet of pilgrims, trekkers, ponies and yaks. Across the valley, on the northern side of the arid Jhong Khola, can be seen the ruins of Dzong, at one time the

The village of Muktinath below the Pilgrim Shrine

most important village in this corner of the mountains and seat of the local ruler. (Another name for the tributary stream below is Dzong Khola, named after this village.) Above Muktinath, village and shrine, the route to the Thorong La which is crossed on the Annapurna Circuit, bears right into the nearby obvious valley, but the pass itself cannot be seen from here. Downvalley a wonderful view shows Dhaulagiri hovering pristine white on a far horizon. Catch it at sunset if you can.

The sacred shrine of Muktinath is located a short distance above the village in a poplar grove. To Buddhists as to Hindus it is very much a place of salvation. There is a small Buddhist *gompa* and a Hindu temple dedicated to Vishnu. Around the temple walls springs have been diverted to form 108 water spouts which hold mysteries of life and death, and which grant salvation to believers who bathe there. In the *gompa* jets of natural gas produce a constant flame beside a spring of water: one of the miracles of Muktinath, attributed to Brahma, the creator-god.

RETURN ROUTES TO POKHARA

Unless your plan is to cross the Thorong La above Muktinath and descend through the valley of the Marsyangdi, in effect reversing the Annapurna Circuit trek described earlier in this book (not recommended in a clockwise direction), your return to Pokhara will naturally be a reversal of most of the upward route through the Kali Gandaki. For a description of this route, if needed, please refer to the Circuit trek, Stage 10 onwards. However, there are some variations that could be made and these are briefly outlined below.

1) Muktinath to Tukuche; east bank route. (1½ days)

Instead of returning to Kagbeni, stay on the main trail below **KHINGAR**. This remains high, climbs through a rock band and rounds a spur of hillside (superb views), before descending to **EKLEBHATTI**. From here to **JOMOSOM** is the same as the upward route, but below Jomosom keep on the left bank of the river (east side) on a trail that goes to **THINIGAON** at the mouth of the valley which leads to the Tilicho La. Continue to **DHUMPHA**, where you could cross to the west bank near **MARPHA**, or carry on through **CHAIRA** (see the Tibetan carpet weavers here) and **CHIMANG** (Chhimgaon) before recrossing to the main trail again north of **TUKUCHE**.

2) Larjung to Kalopani; west bank route. (2-2½ hours)

The standard trail crosses to the east (left) bank below Larjung, on the large suspension bridge reached a few minutes south of the Ghatte Khola. However, there is another trail which remains on the west bank. It crosses two more tributaries immediately below Dhaulagiri, and leads directly to **KALOPANI**.

3) Tatopani to Pokhara via Beni. (3-4 days)

This alternative to the well-trekked, but tiring, route across the Poon Hill Danda may not be as scenically interesting, but it offers another view of the middle hill country north-west of Pokhara. Be warned, though, that it can be a very warm trek in springtime. It diverts from the standard route south of Tatopani, just after you cross the Ghar Khola. Instead of turning uphill by the tea-houses, continue down-valley on the left bank of the river. Cross to the right bank (west side) at **TIPLYAN** and continue downstream as far as **BENI** (about 7 hours from Tatopani). Leaving Beni cross the Kali Gandaki again and walk down-valley on its left bank all the way to **KUSMA. POKHARA** lies about two days walk to the east, and may be reached by way of **TILHAR, THAMARJUNG** and **NAUDANDA**. (It is possible to take a bus or taxi from Suikhet, below Naudanda, into Pokhara.)

4) Ghorapani to Pokhara via Ghandrung. (3 days)

This is another fine option which provides beautiful views of Machhapuchhare and a hint of the wonders to be found within the Sanctuary. From **GHORAPANI DEURALI** head up onto the eastern ridge and follow a severe switchback trail by way of **DEURALI** and **BANTHANTI** to the viewpoint and lodge settlement of **TADAPANI**. A steep descent from here takes you down to **GHANDRUNG**, home of the ACAP headquarters and a scenic place in which to spend the night. From Ghandrung descend to the Modi Khola and climb on the other side to **LANDRUNG**, continue over a wooded ridge to **DHAMPUS** and from there head down to **POKHARA**. (Transport is available near Suikhet, below Dhampus.)

OTHER TREK IDEAS

Those treks already described in detail have justifiably become very popular, and as such plenty of traditional *bhattis* have been modified along the trails to accommodate Western trekkers. However, the populated middle hills, though less dramatic than those of the higher mountains, provide a wealth of opportunities for those who are keen to experience the unchanged Nepal where there are few, if any, trekker's lodges and where a smattering of basic Nepali will be helpful in getting around. A tent and a porter-guide will enable you to travel for days or even weeks among these hills, still enjoying views that contrast a foreground of lush cultivated farmland with the great snow mountains that seem to line every northern horizon. To journey along uncluttered pathways from village to village that have seen only a comparative handful of foreign visitors is to gain a fresh insight into the ways of this ancient kingdom.

To east and west of Pokhara numerous trails exist to entice the inquisitive trekker, and to the north-east too routes explore the unsung valleys and ridges that lead towards Lamjung Himal. Any trails south of a line running roughly from Pokhara to Beni will be uncomfortably hot during the immediate pre- and post-monsoon periods, but would be fine from late October onwards. Study available maps and start dreaming. But remember, trails marked on the maps represent only a few of the routes in daily use. Allow these merely to serve as an inspiration for dreams and as a spur to adventure.

As a halfway option between the popular and the largely unknown ways, variations of those treks previously described - especially combining approach routes to the Sanctuary with those at the southern end of the Kali Gandaki and Ghar Khola valleys - will seldom be trekked alone, but are certainly worth considering too.

But one of the finest long treks neighbouring the Annapurna region, whilst still being accessible from Pokhara, is that which makes a close study of Dhaulagiri. Instead of viewing this giant mountain from the Kali Gandaki, as on the Pilgrim's Trail and Annapurna Circuit, the approach to its Base Camp explores country farther to the west: in the valley which penetrates to the very heart of the massif, between Dhaulagiri I and the assembled group of Dhaulagiris II, III, IV and V.

Dhaulagiri Base Camp Trek: (21 days)

A there-and-back trek from Pokhara to the Base Camp site at 4750m (15,584ft) beside the Chhonbardan Glacier at the head of the Myagdi Khola valley, would take about three weeks, although extra days should be allowed for side trips and to aid acclimatisation. It is a very fine trek on which it will be necessary to carry food and camping equipment for several days. Although there will most likely be other trekking parties on the trail, it is nowhere as busy as the Annapurna routes already described. There is also an opportunity for experienced and well-acclimatised groups to make a full circuit of the mountain. This is also briefly outlined below as Dhaulagiri Inner Circuit.

The trek begins by sharing the Pilgrim's Trail as far as **NAUDANDA**, then breaks away westward through **PANDOR** and **BANE KHARKA** to **THAMARJUNG**. Next day leads south along a ridge, then drops to the Modi Khola, crosses to the right bank and climbs to **CHUWA**, passes through **KUSMA** and enters the lower reaches of the Kali Gandaki valley. At **BENI** the Kali Gandaki is joined by the Myagdi Khola, a major river system flowing from the north-west, and it is this river that is followed to its headwaters in the next nine or ten days.

From Beni the trail remains on the left bank (north side) for the best part of two days, as far as **DARBANG**. A suspension bridge then crosses to the true right bank where you soon begin a long day's climb upvalley with some superb views to Dhaulagiri. On Day 7 the way crosses a major tributary, the Dhara Khola, and turns northward along the right (west) bank of the Myagdi Khola. Passing into the valley's stern gorge, in two days go through **JYARDAN** and on to **DOBANG**.

The route heads between the massive flanks of Dhaulagiri I and those of Dhaulagiri V as the valley curves to the north-east and is choked with the Chhonbardan Glacier. The Base Camp site looks directly onto the North Face of Dhaulagiri I, and at ice-plastered flanks soaring overhead, a dramatic place from which to study the world of high mountains. From Pokhara to this point demands about 12 days of walking.

Dhaulagiri Inner Circuit: (21 days)

In order to achieve a circuit of the mountain, those trekkers with necessary equipment (ice axes, crampons and ropes) and sufficient experience in their use could continue their trek by climbing above the Base Camp site to reach **FRENCH PASS** (5360m: 17,585ft), descending into Hidden Valley (so-named by members of Herzog's 1950 Annapurna expedition) and then crossing **DHAMPUS PASS** (5250m: 17,224ft) between Tukuche Peak and Thapa Peak. This latter pass gives access to the Kali Gandaki's valley at **TUKUCHE**, from which point you follow the down-valley route of the Annapurna Circuit trek for the next five days to **POKHARA**.

This Circuit makes a serious challenge. Glacier skills are called for to climb from Dhaulagiri Base Camp to French Pass, and between this point and the last part of the descent to Tukuche difficulties could arise in the event of poor visibility. The trail is not always clear, but when conditions are good and views unhindered by cloud, it makes a stunningly beautiful expedition.

Jomosom to Mustang Trek: (12-14 days)

A less-strenuous trek than the Dhaulagiri Circuit is that which visits the fabled, long-forbidden kingdom of Mustang upstream of Kagbeni in the upper valley of the Kali Gandaki. Less-strenuous it may be, but the rewards are plentiful, for until very recently only a small handful of foreigners had ever visited Mustang, and even now the Nepalese government has placed a strict limit on the number of trekkers allowed in. Regulations also restrict visitors to members of organised trekking groups; a high fee (US$500 per week in 1992) is charged to each trekker for a special permit, and groups must carry all food and cooking fuel and be accompanied by a liaison officer. The normal start and end to this trek is Jomosom, on the Pilgrim's Trail. Jomosom is reached by air from Pokhara, weather conditions permitting.

From **JOMOSOM** the trek takes about six days to reach the incredible walled town of **LO MANTHANG**, which sits at an altitude of about 3700m (12,140ft). The route passes through **KAGBENI** and **CHELE**, then on the west side of the valley to **EKLOBHATTI** and **TSARANG**, passing old forts and a fascinating landscape of wind-eroded cliffs. Time should be allowed for exploring Lo Manthang and the country further north along the Mustang Khola, and then an alternative return can be made to Jomosom by way of **TANGE, TETANG** and **MUKTINATH**.

Trek leaders Bob Gibbons and Sian Pritchard-Jones were among the first to visit Lo Manthang after it was opened for groups, and they have produced a valuable guidebook to the trail. *Mustang - A Trekking Guide* is published (1993) in Kathmandu by Tiwari's Pilgrims Book House. See also *Mustang The Forbidden Kingdom* by Michel Peissel, *Journey to Mustang* by Guiseppe Tucci, and *Trek to Mustang* by Stan Armington.

The Manaslu Circuit: (20-23 days)

The Manaslu Himal rises as a beautiful wall of snow peaks to the east of the Marsyangdi and is seen on several of the early stages of the Annapurna Circuit. The north and western flanks are drained by the Dudh Khola (which empties into the Marsyangdi at Dharapani), the eastern slopes by the Buri Gandaki. The two valleys are joined by the Larkya La (5213m; 17,103ft), from both sides of which magnificent high mountains, snowfields and glaciers are laid out for inspection.

The Manaslu Circuit is, like the Mustang Trek, subject to tight controls and a limitation of 400 trekkers a year. Only *bona-fide* groups may apply for permits; a liaison officer has to be employed, and a minimum-impact code complied with in order to protect the environment and culture of villages en route. The trek is an outstanding one.

GORKHA, reached by road from Kathmandu, makes an obvious starting point. From the foothill ridge above it a stunning view north leads the eye beyond countless intervening crests to the line of Peak 29, Himalchuli and Baudha Peak. To the north-west stands Annapurna II, to the north-east Ganesh Himal. The trek crosses foothill country to **ARUGHAT BAZAAR**, then heads upstream through the gorges of the Buri Gandaki to the upper reaches of the valley on the northern side of the Himalayan Divide. Here villagers who live in **LHOGAON, SAMAGAON** and **SAMDO** are of Tibetan stock; the Tibetan border runs along the northern walling mountains.

Crossing the **LARKYA LA** is not particularly arduous from the east, and the descent through the valley of the Dudh Khola is a delight in every step. At **DHARAPANI** the Annapurna Circuit is joined, and the busy trail followed downvalley for two days as far as **KHUDI**. It would then be possible to cross the foothills heading south-east to **GORKHA** to complete the circuit, or three days south-west to **SISUWA** at the roadhead where a bus can be taken as far as **POKHARA**.

APPENDIX A: ROUTE SUMMARIES

Route	Distance	Height gain/loss	Time	Page
The Pilgrim's Trail to Muktinath				
1: Pokhara-Lumle-Birethanti	24kms 918m	(-640m)	5½-6 hrs	134
2: Birethanti-Ulleri	7kms	976m	4-4½ hrs	137
3: Ulleri-Ghorapani	5kms	782m	3-3½ hrs	138
4: Ghorapani-Sikha-Tatopani	14kms	-1682m	4½-5 hrs	140
5: Tatopani-Dana-Ghasa	12kms	824m	4½-5 hrs	143
6: Ghasa-Tukuche	15kms	578m	5½ hrs	145
7: Tukuche-Jomosom-Kagbeni	20kms	213m	5 hrs	150
8: Kagbeni-Muktinath	9kms	998m	3-3½ hrs	154

APPENDIX B: TREKKING PEAKS IN THE ANNAPURNA REGION

As has been mentioned already the term 'Trekking Peak' is something of a misnomer, for although their summits are not among the most difficult for climbers in the Himalaya, the 18 mountains included in the list drawn up by the Nepal Mountaineering Association (NMA) are beyond the dreams or abilities of most trekkers. Measuring between 5500 metres (18,045ft) and 6600 metres (21,654ft) these peaks demand a certain expertise and provide climbing adventure which slots somewhere between alpine and high peak expeditionary mountaineering. Of course, one or two of those on the list are much easier than others, and if tackled under good conditions may seem rather 'tame' to climbers with a few epic alpine experiences behind them. However, in the Himalaya as in the Alps, conditions can vary enormously and what might be a straightforward four-day ascent one week can easily turn into a nightmare of life-threatening proportions the next.

Trekking peaks, as opposed to full-scale expedition peaks, are subject to a minimum of formalities and expense. Application is made first to the NMA (P.O. Box 1435, Naxal, Hattisar, Kathmandu). On completion of an application form and payment of a modest fee, in foreign currency by cash or travellers cheques, a permit for a period of one month is granted, and an approved sirdar must then be employed to accompany the climbing party for the duration of the trek/climb. A full list of climbing rules is set out in a booklet available from the NMA at the above address.

The official list of Trekking Peaks is grouped according to height; those of 6000 metres and above are in Group A, while those of less than 6000 metres are listed in Group B. Climbing fees for peaks in Group A are double that of Group B. The list covers a wide geographical area, but those within the region covered by this guide are given below. Bill O'Connor's comprehensive book on *The Trekking Peaks of Nepal* is highly recommended to anyone planning to tackle one of these peaks. It is widely available in specialist bookshops in the West as well as in those of Kathmandu.

Manang Himal:

Three Trekking Peaks contained in Group A are reached by a trek through the Marsyangdi valley. These are Chulu West (6419m: 21,060ft), Chulu East (6200m: 20,341ft) and Pisang Peak (6091m: 19,984ft).

Much confusion surrounds the altitude and, indeed, the actual location of the Chulu peaks. O'Connor points out that several summits forming part of the massif are not shown on maps of the region, while altitudes quoted for those that are, are considered suspect. However, as an arena for climbing adventure there is plenty of scope, with two possible summits to aim for on the **CHULU WEST** permit, and another two on that for **CHULU EAST**. Various routes have already been made and O'Connor outlines them in his book. Base Camp for Chulu West is approached from Manang, while that for Chulu East is reached by way of Hongde through the valley of the Chegagji Khola.

PISANG PEAK is climbed by a long snow slog and is best approached from Pisang village, from which it appears seriously foreshortened. It is a large bulk of a mountain tapering to a neat snow pyramid, and was first climbed solo in 1955 by a member of a German expedition heading for Annapurna. From the upper slopes a magnificent view is afforded of the Annapurna range to the south and west across the deep trench of the Marsyangdi valley.

Annapurna Himal:

Situated within the Annapurna Sanctuary, or located on its rim, four peaks are on the NMA list. Hiunchuli and Singu Chuli, both being above 6000 metres, are contained within Group A, while Tharpu Chuli and Mardi Himal are in Group B.

HIUNCHULI (6441m: 21,132ft) forms the western 'gatepost' of the Sanctuary. Seen from the south it appears as a large snow-bound extension of Annapurna South, while from the north it is a graceful mountain with sharply defined ridges rising to a pointed summit. It is not an easy peak; the original South-east Face route is plagued with rockfall and avalanche potential, while the North-west Face offers steep ice and enticing couloirs.

SINGU CHULI, otherwise known as Fluted Peak (6501m: 21,329ft), received its first ascent in 1957 from Wilfred Noyce and David Cox whilst acclimatising for their attempt on Machhapuchhare. It rises to the east of Annapurna I and overlooks the neighbouring trekking peak of Tharpu Chuli. An attractive mountain, it has several difficult routes and nowhere offers an easy option.

THARPU CHULI, or Tent Peak (5663m: 18,579ft) forms the southern end of a ridge projecting into the Annapurna basin from Glacier Dome (Tarke Kang). It's another fine-looking mountain whose original name is easy to understand when seen from Annapurna Base Camp, but whose height is debatable. Jimmy Roberts, the first Westerner to penetrate the Sanctuary, made an attempt to climb Tharpu Chuli in 1956, but it was not until 1964 that the summit was at last reached by a Japanese expedition. There are clearly many new routes to be tried, in addition to the three already recorded.

Finally, **MARDI HIMAL** (5587m: 18,330ft) is the close south-western neighbour of Machhapuchhare and is almost completely dominated by the loftier 'fish-tail' peak. Although it is so close to the Annapurna Sanctuary (it forms part of the eastern wall of the Modi Khola's gorge), Mardi Himal is reached by a difficult five-day trek from Pokhara along a ridge that overlooks the Mardi Khola. The actual climb, following the route of the first ascent made by Jimmy Roberts in 1961, is not difficult under normal conditions and has an alpine grade of F *(facile)*.

APPENDIX C: USEFUL ADDRESSES

1: Selected Overseas Missions of the Nepalese Government:
Embassies:

U.K.
12a Kensington Palace Gardens
London W8 4QU (Tel: 071 229 1594)

U.S.A.
2131 Leroy Place
Washington
DC 20008 (Tel: 202 6674550)

France
7 Rue de Washington
75008 Paris (Tel: 43592861)

Germany
Im-Hag 15
Bad Godesberg 2
D-5300 Bonn
(Tel: 0228 343097)

Consulates:
820 Second Avenue
Suite 202
New York
NY 10017
USA (Tel: 212 3704188)

473 Jackson Street
San Francisco
CA 94111
USA (Tel: 415 4341111)

310 Dupont Street
Toronto
Ontario
Canada (Tel: 416 9687252)

870 Military Road
Suite 1 Strand Centre
Mosman, Sydney
NSW 2088
Australia (Tel: 9603565)

2: Selected Foreign Missions in Nepal:

British Embassy
Lainchaur
Kathmandu (Tel: 411789/410583)

American Embassy
Pani Pokhari
Kathmandu
(Tel: 411179/411601)

Australian Embassy
Bhat Bhatani
Kathmandu (Tel: 411578)

The following countries also have Embassies located in Kathmandu:

China: Baluwatar
Germany: Kantipath
Israel: Lazimpat
Japan: Pani Pokhari
Korea (South): Tahachal

France: Lazimpat
India: Lainchaur
Italy: Baluwatar
Korea (North): Patan
Pakistan: Pani Pokhari
Thailand:Thapathali

The following countries also have Kathmandu-based Consulates:

Austria: Kupondole
Denmark: Kantipath
Netherlands: Kumaripati
Switzerland: Jawalakhel

Belgium: Lazimpat
Finland: Khichpokhari
Sweden: Khichpokhari

In addition the following Cultural Centres are based in Kathmandu:

The British Council
Kantipath (Tel: 211305)

French Cultural Centre
Bag Bazar (Tel: 214326)

United States Information Service
New Road (Tel: 211250)

3: Conservation Organisations in Nepal:
Annapurna Conservation Area Project
ACAP Headquarters
Ghandruk Village
Ghandruk Village Panchayat
Kaski District
Nepal

King Mahendra Trust for
   Nature Conservation
KMTNC
PO Box 3712
Babar Mahal
Kathmandu
Nepal

4: Map Suppliers:
Edward Stanford Ltd
12-14 Long Acre
London
WC2E 9LP

Bradt Enterprises Inc
95 Harvey Street
Cambridge
MA 02140 USA

Michael Chessler Books
PO Box 2436
Evergreen
CO 80439 USA

There are also many book sellers in Kathmandu and Pokhara who stock trekking maps for the Annapurna region.

APPENDIX D: GLOSSARY

Whilst it would be possible to trek the main trails of Annapurna speaking only English, a litle effort to communicate with Nepalis in their own language will be amply repaid. If you are trekking with an organised group plenty of opportunities will arise to practise a few words and phrases with your crew and porters. Tea-house trekkers will find that some attempt to speak the language will be appreciated by lodge-keepers and the owners of tea-houses along the trail, while those who employ a porter-guide will discover that mutual language-exchange is a valuable bonus to the day-to-day pleasures of the trail. Nepalis who meet and work with Europeans are keen to expand their vocabulary, and are usually very happy to offer some instruction in their own language in return for help given in English.

The following glossary lists a few words that may be useful on the trail. However, there are a few Nepali phrasebooks and dictionaries available that would be worth consulting, in addition to Stephen Bezruchka's highly recommended language tape and accompanying book, *Nepali for Trekkers* (The Mountaineers 1991). Lonely Planet publish a small, lightweight *Nepal Phrasebook* that would sit easily in a shirt pocket for instant use on the trail.

aaja	- today
baato	- trail
baayaan	- left (direction)
banthanti	- the place in the forest
bazaar	- market
bhatti	- traditional inn or guest-house
bholi	- tomorrow
Bhot	- Tibet
Bhotyia	- Buddhist people of mountain Nepal
bistaari	- slowly
chang	- home-made beer
charpi	- latrine
chautaara	- trailside platform for resting porters' loads
chaulki	- police post
chini	- sugar
chiso paani	- cold water
chiyaa	- tea
chorten	- Buddhist shrine, like an elaborate cairn
daahine	- right (direction)
daal bhaat	- staple meal of Nepal: rice (bhaat) with lentil sauce (daal)
danda	- ridge
deurali	- a pass on a ridge
dhai	- yoghurt
dhara	- waterspout
dharmsala	- pilgrims' rest house
dokan	- shop (see also pasal)
doko	- porter's conical basket for carrying loads
dudh	- milk
ghar	- house
gompa	- Buddhist temple
goth	- herdsman's shelter
hijo	- yesterday
himal	- snow mountain

kani	- covered archway, decorated with Buddhist motifs
khaana	- food
kharka	- high pasture
khola	- river
khukari	- Gurkha knife with curved blade
kot	- fortress
la	- high pass
lama	- Buddhist monk or priest
lekh	- hill or foothill ridge
maasu	- meat
maati baato	- upper trail
mani	- Buddhist prayer; from the mantra "om mani padme hum"
mani wall	- stone wall carved with Buddhist prayers
mantra	- religious incantation
namaste	- traditional greeting; it means "I salute the God within you"
nun	- salt
paani	- water (see also chiso paani, taato paani and umaleko paani)
pasal	- shop (see also dokan)
phedi	- literally "the place at the foot of the hill"
phul	- egg
pokhari	- lake
rakshi	- distilled spirit
roti	- bread
sadhu	- Hindu ascetic
shaligram	- ammonite
sidha	- straight ahead (direction)
sirdar	- man in charge of trek crew (porters, guides and kitchen staff)
stupa	- large chorten
taato paani	- hot water
tal	- lake
Thakali	- people of the Thak Khola, the upper region of the Kali Gandaki
thanka	- Buddhist scroll painting
thanti	- place
thukpa	- noodle soup
tsampa	- roasted barley flour
ukaalo	- steep uphill
umaleko paani	- boiled water

Days of the Week

Aitobar	- Sunday	Bihibaar	- Thursday
Sombaar	- Monday	Sukrobaar	- Friday
Mangalbaar	- Tuesday	Sanibaar	- Saturday
Budhbaar	- Wednesday		

Numbers

1	- ek	25	- pachhis
2	- dui	30	- tis
3	- tin	35	- paitis
4	- char	40	- chaalis
5	- paanch	45	- paitaalis
6	- chha	50	- pachaas
7	- saat	55	- pachpanna
8	- aath	60	- saathi
9	- nau	65	- paisatthi
10	- das	70	- sattari
11	- eghaara	75	- pachahattar
12	- baahra	80	- asi
13	- tehra	85	- pachaasi
14	- chaudha	90	- nabbe
15	- pandhra	95	- panchaanaabbe
16	- sohra	100	- ek sae
17	- satra	1000	- ek hajaar
18	- athaara		
19	- unnaais		
20	- bis		

BIBLIOGRAPHY

There is no shortage of books on Nepal, but those listed below have specific interest to trekkers concentrating on the Annapurna region. Several have wider scope, of course, but all contain information relevant to our needs. Some inevitably are out of print and unobtainable in the West, except through public libraries. However, many bookshops in Kathmandu stock an admirable selection of new, old and reprinted volumes, and will be worth investigating if you cannot obtain what you require at home.

1: General Tourist Guides:

The number of general tourist guides to Nepal is growing. Perhaps the best and most comprehensive on the market at present is:
Insight Guide: Nepal edited by Hans Höfer (APA Publications). Expert contributions, both textual and photographic, give this regularly-updated book an air of authority.

Others, with similar emphasis on photographic appeal, include *The Insider's Guide to Nepal* by Brian Tetley (Moorland Publishing Co 1991) and *Nepal* (Nelles Guides published by Nelles Verlag/Robertson McCarta 1990).

Not a tourist guide as such, the following large format coffee-table book is packed with an assortment of information and photographs gleaned from the author's wide-ranging travels throughout the country. Toni Hagen was the first man to be given the freedom to explore the whole of Nepal and as such his knowledge of the country must be considered unique. *Nepal: The Kingdom of the Himalayas* by Toni Hagen (Kümmerley and Frey 1980) is highly recommended.

Nepal - A Travel Survival Kit by Tony Wheeler & Richard Everist (Lonely Planet 1990) gives lots of practical information on getting around Nepal and includes an introduction to trekking.

2: Trekking:

Practically every trekking guide to focus on Nepal attempts to cover as many areas as possible. Each one contains much of interest and practical use, but for the majority of trekkers whose visit concentrates on one route or one region only, there will inevitably be large passages of unused material contained in them.

Trekking in Nepal by Stephen Bezruchka (Cordee/The Mountaineers - 6th edition 1991). This is *the* classic trekker's guide; packed with valuable information, sensitively written and regularly revised, all prospective visitors should study this book before leaving home. Invaluable. The author's love of the country and concern for its people is a shining example to all who follow in his footsteps.

Trekking in the Nepal Himalaya by Stan Armington (Lonely Planet - 5th edition 1991). A compact guide to five regions of Nepal including, of course, Annapurna. The author has spent many years leading trekking parties in the Himalaya, and now lives in Kathmandu.

Trekking in Nepal, West Tibet and Bhutan by Hugh Swift (Sierra Club/ Hodder & Stoughton 1989). An interesting overview of the trekking possibilities in these three countries, it covers too much territory to give precise detail, but makes enjoyable reading.

Trekking in Nepal by Toru Nakano (Springfield Books - latest edition 1990). Brief route descriptions, regional maps and lots of colour photos, this is a translation from the Japanese original. The photographs will remind you to take a camera and plenty of film.

Adventure Treks: Nepal by Bill O'Connor (Crowood Press 1990 now Cicerone Press). Personal narratives of several treks including Annapurna Circuit and Sanctuary. Not a guidebook as such, it conveys some of the magic, as well as some of the frustrations, of trekking.

The Trekking Peaks of Nepal by Bill O'Connor (Crowood Press - latest edition 1991). This companion volume to Adventure Treks is, perhaps, of more value, even if you have no intention of climbing any of these peaks. Brief details of major trekking routes are given, as well as the main purpose of the book, which is to outline possibilities for climbing on all 18 nominated "trekking peaks".

Mustang - A Trekking Guide by Bob Gibbons and Sian Pritchard-Jones

(Tiwari's Pilgrims Book House 1993) for anyone planning to visit this magical region north of Kagbeni.

Trekking: Great Walks of the World by John Cleare (Unwin Hyman 1988) contains a lively, well-illustrated chapter about the Annapurna Circuit.

Classic Walks of the World edited by Walt Unsworth (Oxford Illustrated Press 1985) also includes a chapter on the Annapurna Circuit.

3: Mountains & Mountaineering:

Annapurna by Maurice Herzog (Jonathan Cape 1952). Herzog's account of the first ascent of an 8000m peak is a true mountaineering classic, and will be of great interest to anyone planning to tackle the Circuit or the Pilgrim's Trail; interesting to match the author's descriptions of the Kali Gandaki valley and villages with your own experience.

Nepal Himalaya by H.W.Tilman (Cambridge University Press 1952, now contained in a collection of *The Seven Mountain Travel Books* published by Diadem Books/The Mountaineers 1983). Tilman visited Manang in 1950 and made an attempt on Annapurna IV. Contains good descriptions of the Marsyangdi valley and of the peaks that wall it.

Climbing the Fish's Tail by Wilfred Noyce (Heinemann 1958). Account of the only expedition to climb on Machhapuchhare, it provides a stimulating picture of the Sanctuary.

Annapurna South Face by Chris Bonington (Cassell 1971). Bonington's team climbed the impressive South Face in 1970, thus heralding a new era in Himalayan mountaineering. Of especial interest to those planning to trek into the Sanctuary.

4: Travel & Exploration:

Cloud-Dwellers of the Himalayas by Windsor Chorlton (Time-Life Books 1982) describes life in Nar-Phu, the remote region of Manang District.

Himalayan Pilgrimage by David Snellgrove (Prajna Press 1981). Travels through then-remote parts of Nepal in the 1950s, including Annapurna. Interesting descriptions, especially of the *gompa* at Braga on the Annapurna Circuit trek.

5: Anthropology & Natural History:

Birds of Nepal by Fleming, Fleming and Bangdel (Avalok 1984). A comprehensive field guide, richly illustrated.

A Popular Guide to the Birds and Mammals of the Annapurna Conservation Area (ACAP 1989)

Concise Flowers of the Himalaya by Oleg Polunin and Adam Stainton (Oxford University Press 1987)

Butterflies of Nepal by Colin Smith (Tecpress 1989)

People of Nepal by Dor Bahadur Bista (Ratna Pustak Bhandar - 5th edition 1987). Background information on a number of ethic groups of Nepal.

The Festivals of Nepal by Mary M.Anderson (George Allen & Unwin 1971)

Printed by CARNMOR PRINT & DESIGN, 95-97 LONDON ROAD, PRESTON, LANCASHIRE, UK.